Profiles in Mormon Courage

INSPIRING STORIES *of*
STALWART AND STEADFAST INDIVIDUALS
in LATTER-DAY SAINT HISTORY

❧

HARTT WIXOM

CFI
SPRINGVILLE, UT

© 2007 Hartt Wixom

ISBN 13: 978-1-55517-852-9

Published by CFI, an imprint of Cedar Fort, Inc.,
2373 W. 700 S., Springville, UT, 84663
Distributed by Cedar Fort, Inc. www.cedarfort.com

LIBRARY OF CONGRESS CATALOGING-IN-PUBLICATION DATA

Wixom, Hartt.
  Profiles in Mormon courage / Hartt Wixom.
    p. cm.
  ISBN 978-1-55517-852-9
  1. Mormons--Biography. I. Title.

  BX8693.W59 2007
  289.3092'2--dc22
  [B]

                                        2007004923

Edited and typeset by Angela Olsen
Cover design by Nicole Williams
Cover design © 2007 by Lyle Mortimer

Printed in the United States of America

10 9 8 7 6 5 4 3 2 1

Printed on acid-free paper

Table of Contents

Foreword

It was said best on the Oprah Winfrey television show of 30 January 2003: "Talk to your ancestors. Ask them, am I doing what you hoped I would? For what purpose did you suffer and sacrifice for your unknown posterity?"

These are questions for all to ponder. What better way to show our gratitude for those sacrifices—written that we might know of their love and concern for us—than to share with our own posterity our hopes, dreams, and our fulfilling experiences, as they have done?

Obviously, the stories within these pages would not be known to us today if someone had not cared enough to record the events. Keeping a diary or journal (then or now) is not only a vital, but it would seem a *sacred* obligation.

But some might say, "I can't write; I've done nothing worth writing about." Are we then exempt? Elder Gerald Lund of the Seventy once said at a Pioneer Day address on 20 July 2002: "The extraordinary things said and done by our ancestors were said and done by ordinary people. Just like us today."

One thing we can all do is tell our own story. For those who are Latter-day Saints, it is especially important to share with our posterity what struggles we have overcome or are working through to gain a testimony and to live the principles of the restored gospel.

Writing about ourselves is hardly self-centered. How can it be when we share with others our feelings about the many ways the spirit of Jesus Christ has strengthened our lives and has helped us meet difficult challenges? And how can they know if we don't write it down, as did our forefathers?

Many profound historical gems have been recorded—by ordinary people—in personal journals. It is especially thrilling in any family research to read of an event, written in official history books, and then to see it personalized in an ancestor's journal. This could go something like this anecdote from Enoch B. Tripp: "I saw with my own eyes in Nauvoo the visage of Joseph Smith upon the countenance of Brigham Young as he spoke to us about who should be the next president of the church." Enoch B. Tripp's story, shared in chapter one, provides valuable clues into what it was like as a non-Mormon, to enter the Mormon city of Nauvoo at a time when it was being besieged by other non-Mormons. Tripp was so enamored of what he saw that despite many lies he was told about the Mormons, he himself was converted.

The value of oral history must also be taken into account. The following story was given to me verbally about my great grandmother, Lois Orenia Wixom: "My son returned home with a sack of flour which he said fell off a wagon; he must find the owner. "Oh, no," I said. "We have been going hungry for days and I've been praying for help. You can't take that flour back. I prayed it here." The story was told to me by Ruth Widdison, co-author of *A Wixom Family History*. But alas, it is secondhand, and not finding it written down with any reference, I have no way to check it for accuracy. I do not include it in the pages ahead, but it is given here to suggest that some of our ancestors may well have had a rich sense of humor as well as a great devotion to deity from which we could all profitably emulate.

On the other hand, a process such as locating, deciphering, and writing from family histories can carry a few pitfalls. Family chroniclers often slip into subjectivity, such as this entry in the author's own family history: "My mother's children had no bad habits." (Quick, take them into the celestial kingdom before they do.) Or, a zealous descendent may say this for posterity, which can be just as frustrating: "She told of the many exciting things which happened to her as she sailed to America and crossed the plains." And then fails to mention any.

It may also be true that family histories tend not to tell the entire story about a deceased loved one. Perhaps a relative has become even more beloved and is deemed more righteous simply by being deceased. The biographer who follows must then do more than rely solely on family histories; he must corroborate the stories with other sources such as journals of peers, histories of the period, and newspaper clippings. Many may be located in a long neglected library archive.

Some of us may even include error in our writings such as the following: "Many died due to their faith in going to Zion." Yet, the record may show they died before or well after the journey to Zion. We should, of course, make every effort to be accurate and provide examples and sources to support our conclusions.

Sifting truth from error within these pages is the author's responsibility, of course, and is taken seriously. All referenced sources are listed at the end of each chapter, to assist the reader in determining historical accuracy, as it is true that faith-promoting rumors do little to engender trust. In this book, the author has meticulously examined anecdotes given to separate fact from fiction. Sometimes, as is evident in the history of W. W. Phelps, the facts reflect human weakness. But in Phelps's case, it is gratifying to see how he overcame that weakness with renewed faith and purpose.

We can greatly bless our posterity by keeping accurate journals to show how *we* met the many challenges we face almost daily. To be sure, our trials today do not include following a creaking wagon across dusty trails or battling hostile mobs. But as any parent in Zion can attest, we have our own crosses to bear today: the availability of drugs, the prevalance of sex and violence on TV and in the movies, and other adversities of the modern era. We all need examples, if not heroes to meet these challenges. Many are found in the pages ahead.

Those selected have much to offer us. Some of the pioneers portrayed herein have never had their life stories mentioned in print. For others, like Ephraim Hanks and W. W. Phelps, what follows is "The Rest of the Story," in Paul Harvey fashion.

Take Ephraim Hanks for example. He not only saved many lives by bringing in food and clothing to dying handcart pioneers, but saved many lives by administering to the sick. He was truly an extraordinary man. But where and how did he gain the resolve to accomplish what he did? Where did he come from? Where did he go? And that all-important question: what hurdles did he have to overcome to gain the precious virtues that money cannot buy?

Or how can we explain the dramatic turnaround in the life of W. W. Phelps? Once breathing fire and hatred at his brethren, Phelps suddenly expressed a deep sorrow and sought abject forgiveness from these same brethren he had so recently abused. And it came at a time during one of the darkest hours of the church, as enemies closed in on Nauvoo. What was it that so changed his life? Let us find out.

I have attempted nothing more in this book than an honest effort in grasping at the ultimately indefinable something that personifies certain Christian principles which are so capable of dramatically altering lives. The stories included in these pages are here because they exemplify values and virtues which each of us can emulate to lead richer and more abundant lives, no matter our religious persuasion. Each person acquired more than one noble habit, of course; but you will find the featured virtue making a significant difference in that individual's life—twelve virtues we can incorporate into our own lives.

Some are not included in this volume because their stories are already well known, or for the opposite reason: we can find so little about them. That is reason enough to sit down and write our own life stories for the benefit our posterity as well. In the spirit of these pioneer narratives and the love they have shown to us, their posterity, let us go forward to write our own life stories. Let our own spiritual journeys bless our posterity as theirs have ours.

Acknowledgments

I owe the concept of this book to my wife, Judene, who began the research and encouraged my own. She spent many hours proofreading manuscripts to eliminate errors and making valuable suggestions.

I also wish to take a moment to express gratitude that someone took time to write down history in the making for our benefit. I am greatly indebted to the many families who shared previously unpublished diaries and journals left to them by their ancestors. They are listed in the notes at the end of each chapter.

Brigham Young University's Lee Library Special Collections proved most helpful, as well.

Chapter One: Commitment
ENOCH BARTLETT TRIPP

"I felt like it was my duty to be baptized."

Enoch Bartlett Tripp could hardly wait. Like any other businessman, he didn't want to turn down a bargain. He wrote in his journal that while in Cleveland, Ohio, in the late fall of 1845, he read a notice that the Mormons (whoever they might be) were being driven from Nauvoo. They were practically giving away their furniture, farm implements, and homes they had to leave to escape the hostile mobs.

Tripp hurried to Illinois, as he put it, "to make a speculation." After that, he sought to open his own dry goods or shoe repair business somewhat like the one in which his father had prospered.

Unbeknownst to Tripp, his life would never be the same. The twenty-two-year-old Tripp had relatives in the beleaguered city of Nauvoo whom he had never seen, nor they him. He would learn more of the forced exodus from them.

An old photograph of Tripp shows him to be a man of average build with a prominent nose, deep set eyes, high cheek bones, and a full beard. He had made a good start in the dry goods business at home in Maine, but due to a partner's poor management, Tripp found the company in liquidation. He was left with almost nothing. Now wiser, determined not to be taken in again, and with a spirit full of adventure, Tripp set out to start over somewhere else.

Tripp had heard that the Mormons practiced a strange religion, but he vowed not to get involved in it. He would make a polite visit only, buy up all the goods possible at the lowest prices, and move somewhere else to open his own business. But Tripp knew little of what was to come.

Tripp's lengthy written record which he began keeping as a "duty" to future posterity, tells us that en route to Nauvoo, he stopped for the night in Carthage. In talking to townspeople he learned about two Smith brothers who had been shot "in cold blood by a mob armed and painted black." The incident, though a year and a half before, made a strong impression on his young mind.

Sharing here some of the idioms and frontier spelling Tripp used, he says under date of November 1845: "arrived with safety at Carthage & put up at the Stage Hotel for the night. Here is whare the two Smiths wer shot . . . Joseph and Hyrum wer Shot in Cold blood . . . broak into Jail Whar they were awateing . . . upon the 27th day of June 1844."

Tripp learned that "John Taylor was badly wounded but his watch saved his life; the ball hit it, shivered it to pieces. Willard Richards crawled under a bed and escaped. As the mob was breaking in the door and firing, and had already killed Hyrum [Smith], Joseph Smith started to leap from the window and the mob from outside shot him. As he fell dead, these words came from his lips: 'Oh Lord my God.'"

"The friends of the Smiths came from Nauvoo a distance of twenty miles & took their bodies to their city. That was a sad day for the Mormons, for they believed Joseph to be a Prophet of the Lord in this last dispensation & Hyrum a Patriarch over the whole Church."

Adds Tripp: "I know nothing of their religious belief, but it looks to me to be a cold-blooded murder & a big stain upon the state of Illinois & that the mob killed them more on the account of their religious beliefs than they did on the account of being breakers of the Law. If they violated the Law, let them suffer the penalty of that Law & not by the mob."

People in Carthage were still talking about the murders of the Smith brothers because they had just captured Brigham Young—or thought they had, as we shall learn from Tripp's diary. "After taking my supper and returning again to the barroom, I found it filled most full with a hard set of men. Their very countenance looked to me that they would not hesitate long to do most any kind of crime. Their conversation seemed to be principally about the Mormons. They could not find language bad enough to use after them."

The following story is told by Tripp in his diary: "After learning from me of my travels from Maine here & that I was not a Mormon but was intending to visit Nauvoo, they all exclaimed that my life was in great danger there in that place." The men explained that in the Mormon capital men were being "killed in the streets" and thrown into a ditch to steal their clothes. The men kept Tripp up until near midnight telling him "frightful" stories of how the Mormons stole, robbed and murdered for gain.

The desire to go to Nauvoo was great, but it seemed he had blundered into a civil war. Who was right? Well, whoever would win was of no concern to him, except, of course, the opportunity to buy dry goods at reduced prices from a people about to be exiled.

But what about his own safety? He'd already had several harrowing incidents in his recent travels from Maine. In one, a river boat ran aground, marooning him on a sand bar for three days. Another time, a steamboat struck a sandbar, partially sinking. He took a skiff to find help.

Elsewhere, near St. Louis, he declined an invitation to go ashore "for a look at the city." His friend decided to accept. Once out of sight of the boat, the friend met three ruffians who separated him from his money. At another place, Tripp was lured on with prospects of joining a fellow passenger to "share cab expenses"; instead, Tripp found men waiting to rob him. He jumped out and ran into a building, where he overheard someone say, "He's too smart for us." Now, what was he getting himself into?

Shortly before retiring, he was told that a posse of officers had returned from Nauvoo with Brigham Young, the leader of the Mormons. His trial would be held in the morning. There was a great deal of rejoicing among the crowd. Being curious, he decided to witness this impending trial of "Brigham Young."

As he watched, the judge and prosecuting attorney asked the posse leader to bring in the prisoner. "The officer of the posse pointed to a man by him and said, 'there he was.' With all eyes turned upon him, the judge and atty [sic] said that was not Brigham Young but Mr. Miller.'

"Said the posse leader: 'Why did you not tell me that you wasn't Brigham Young?'"

Mr. Miller: "You never asked me." The "bogus Brigham" was released.

At about 10 A.M. Tripp finally gathered enough courage to carry out his mission. Sitting on the mail and passenger stage bound for Nauvoo, Tripp found himself seated next to Mr. Miller.

"I didn't feel in much mood for talking, as my mind was much upon the frightful stories that had been related to me about the Mormons, & I was soon to be in their midst. God only knew what might be my lot."

Mr. Miller "did not seem much in a mood for talking" either. Tripp allowed that Mr. Miller might be a little shaken up, as was he. The two traveled quietly.

"As we neared the city of the Saints so called, I saw men in the distance near the road with guns, which caused me to fear that the reports were true & that these men were out seeking the lives of strangers. My fears were aroused to such a pitch that I kept a lookout upon my right & left & rear to see if there was not some one of them aiming their gun at me to take my life.

"I did not know but the stage driver might be one [Mormon] & take part with these men to take my life. So, I watched them also very close." Mr. Miller was most assuredly a Mormon and if the stage driver was a Mormon as well. . . . Was what the men in Carthage told him true?

Heart in his throat, Tripp asked the stage driver if he knew his Uncle and Aunt Sessions. The driver did not, but he knew their daughter who married W. P. Lyon, a Nauvoo merchant. Tripp tipped the driver fifty cents to take him there before going to the post office.

But instead of seeing men waiting in ambush, he witnessed a memorable scene. "After entering the city on the east, we passed through beautiful streets & . . . came to their temple, which is a beautiful building built of white lime rock which can be seen at a great distance. We then drove down a steep bluff to what they call the River Bottoms and to Mr. W. P. Lyon's store."

Tripp hurried into the store and made immediate inquiry for Mrs. Lyons. "I made myself known to her. She seemed much rejoiced to see me."

Other relatives greeted their long lost relative warmly and "all said I was welcome to make my home with them as long as I saw fit to stay with them . . . which made me feel well." But could he move about the city, away from relatives, without fear?

That night was Christmas Eve, 1845. Since the prophet's death, the city had been continually threatened, but for now, things appeared peaceful. All was calm.

Tripp slept soundly and the next day, being Christmas, it seemed a logical time to talk of things concerning the Christ child. But Tripp writes that concerning their religious affairs, he was determined not to engage in conversation. He would remain "silent."

As Christmas Day moved on, Tripp began to feel more at ease: "The timid feeling that I entered the Mormon city with had in part left me, as I saw that everyone seemed to be attending to their own business & showed no disposition to harm me & being with my cousin [David Sessions, about Tripp's own age] I felt more safe as we rode along. I looked sharp to see if I could see any dead persons by the side of the road, as had been represented to me. I saw none & not so much as any street fighting, which is generally done in cities and villages. All seemed to be in order, peace & quietude."

The newcomer to town visited with a name familiar to Latter-day Saint history students, Patty Sessions. Tripp wrote that his Aunt Patty lived in a log house, "rather on a poor style," on limited property.

Tripp was also introduced to a woman who lived on that property named Rosella Cowing, who was about thirty years of age. "As this people are branded with the name of plurality of wives, I have my suspicions that she is a [plural] wife of Uncle Sessions." That his uncle was practicing polygamy seems to give Tripp pause. What kind of religion was this anyway?

Tripp was further bothered as Christmas Day came to a close. "In the evening, I went with David to the Mormon gathering . . . to see religious folks dance, for I was raised . . . to believe it to be very wicked to dance & now for people professing religion to go & spend the night in dancing, it looks horrible to me. But I am not going to let my prejudice lead me astray. It is an old saying & I believe it a true one & that is, 'Prove all things & hold fast to that which is good.' So if dancing should prove to be good in a religious point of view, I shall be very apt to hold fast to that, for it is an amusement I am very fond of & being taught it is a great sin, it has kept me doing less than I desired." While Tripp's diaries indicate he wanted nothing to do with the strange Mormon religion, based on what he had heard about it, he had grown up in a deeply religious home. Now, as he grew older, he sought to become closer to the God his father had taught him about. In keeping with his father's Free Methodist teachings, Tripp did not want to offend God by drinking, smoking, immodest dress, or by dancing. But was the latter really a sin?

An incident in Tripp's life shows his deep-seated desire to please God. When he was young, he took up with a "spiritual" sect in Maine until finding that they were more of a fraternity than a religion, a social club. "I didn't feel anything," he was later to say. "I didn't feel any closer to my God through my association with them."

Were the Mormons like that, a social group just having fun who didn't care if they offended God by dancing? Was it all right to enjoy the present while preparing for a future life beyond the grave? Tripp would try to keep an open mind. He would see what this strange religion was all about. Christ's spirit and fun? Could one have both?

It seemed to Tripp, as the night wore on, that to the Mormons dancing was more than simply fun. It was a bonding with other Saints, a release from worry and care (and there was plenty of that about), a way of having joy in this life as well as the next, and a chance to cultivate social relations that were most important to a people who loved one another.

Tripp wrote that he found the ballroom filled with "the old & the young & all well clad, full of life and mirth. At the hour appointed, they were all called together, & a prayer was offered up to God, thanking him for all past blessings & mercies & asking his blessings upon them while they were mingling together . . . that no accident might befall them . . . & that nothing might transpire to mar or disturb their happiness. All joined him [the prayer-giver] in saying 'Amen.'"

Tripp was extremely impressed with the orderly proceedings of the night but noted that it seemed "very singular" to ask God's blessing upon them "while they spent the evening sinning" on the dance floor.

Tripp's cousin introduced him to several young ladies. All seemed to be good dancers, wrote Tripp. Good feelings prevailed. "I soon began to feel at home with them, especially after dancing several times with their pretty girls."

Surprisingly, perhaps shockingly, the dance did not let out until four o'clock in the morning. If the community was under stress from the non-Mormon element in late December 1845, Tripp never mentioned it. Perhaps the locals wanted to forget their troubles for a few days.

As 1846 arrived, Tripp spent much time exploring about the countryside with his cousin. "I found the people as a general thing as very kind & benevolent & very intelligent, considering that they were made up of the poor class . . . leaders take much pains to cultivate their minds to usefulness. Brigham Young, Heber C. Kimball & Willard Richards are their present leaders.

"All fears have left me that this people seek my life or the life of any other person that will let them alone & attend to their own business. They are represented the reverse from what they are. In finding this out by experience, I have often asked myself the question, Why are this people so much misrepresented, more especially by the Christian sects of the day . . . there seems to be no people so devoted to their religion as this people appear to be."

Tripp attended some Mormon meetings. They were "conducted in a similar manner to other Christian sects," but Tripp allowed that inasmuch as the members were compelled to soon leave their hard-earned homes, little doctrine was presented. Their principle instruction "was to get ready to leave and how to fit out to do so."

Then, this: "I have always been informed & got the impression upon my mind that they were a duped people & had no minds of their own and were governed and led by their leaders . . . whether it was right or wrong, it was the religion of the people. I found this untrue, as well as all other stories. I find men & women as free to speak & act for themselves here as in other parts of the world. To be sure, they think a great deal of their leaders & strongly believe them to be good men & men of God & true fathers to the people. Seeing all this, it has led me to inquire into their religious beliefs."

While Tripp's interest was kindled, he had to overcome many misconceptions. One was that the Mormons had a Bible of their own, "that they did not believe in the Bible that the other sects of the day do." Tripp learned in time that the Mormons did, indeed, believe in the same Bible as other faiths but he adds: "they believe it reads what it meant."

He soon concluded that the Mormon Church was set up to follow the early Christian organization, and that these latter-day Christians were being persecuted just as Christ and his followers had been in former days. Studying the Apostasy and its meaning to Mormons, he concluded that all the keys of authority to act in God's name had been lost from the earth. Hence the need for a restoration of all that had been lost.

"After many hundred years have rolled away without the Priesthood being upon the earth, God sent Peter, James and John back again to Earth and ordained & bestowed all the keys they were in possession of upon a young man by the name of Joseph Smith. They believe he was a Prophet of God & had organized the Church after the same pattern of the former-day Church & that this was the true Church of Christ, reorganized again upon the Earth with all of its gifts and blessings."

Tripp gives it as his opinion that the devil, the father of all lies, "is now stirring up the hearts of the children of men against the Church of Christ, more especially among the other churches."

Of the Book of Mormon, which he was to learn was another testament of Jesus Christ on the American continent, Tripp soon stated flatly that "the book was translated by Joseph Smith by the gift and power of God. I could see nothing unreasonable in it." He says he found the book easier to understand in points of doctrine than the Bible, "especially that part where Christ appeared to them [ancient Indians or Lamanites] & organized his Church."

Tripp now began reading the Doctrine and Covenants and was impressed "with what a record-keeping people the Mormons are." The book "contains the revelations given through Joseph Smith. I found them all very interesting & instructive."

But Tripp had long held reservations about any religion, anywhere. He was not about to plunge into a mistake. His diary reads upon entry of 1836: "[In this year] a society called Christian Bands got up a great religious excitement in the town of Cambridge . . . many joined their church. Being very young & not understanding the true principles of the Gospel & under the religious excitement of others, I was strongly solicited to join them, to which I consented & was baptized . . .

"But I do not think it ever made any change in me, for after the excitement was over, I cannot say that I felt any change . . . this church could not do miracles like Christ's Church of old, according to the record in the New Testament."

Tripp wrote that while all churches go to the Bible as their guide, "they still fight with one another, saying none are right . . . and none of them live according to the doctrine of Christ & his apostles in the New Testament. "Even in my young days, I began to think the Bible a fable. So, as months & years advanced, I paid less attention to my religious professions but still continued in steady and moral habits & trusted in the future for the best."

After reading and hearing a great deal upon the points of Mormon doctrine, however, he "became convinced that it was the true Church of Christ, if there was any upon the Earth."

Still, Tripp hesitated. He had determined not to be taken in by another religion claiming "God is here." Experience had hardened him and made him wary. Frauds and shams were all around. Even his half brother William, on the surface a Christian believer, had managed to cheat him out of money rightfully his back in Maine. It seems that William had accepted Tripp's horse and saddle in exchange for a promise to teach him the legal profession. But his half-brother never came through. Who could he trust? Another "friend," who wanted to go into business with Tripp, purchased goods on a promise the "friend" didn't keep. Tripp determined that he would not be misled again.

The deciding factor toward baptism for Tripp came in meeting with Church leader Heber C. Kimball, of the First Presidency, at the baptism of Tripp's cousin, who Tripp refers to as Mr. Lyon. "I watched his [Kimball's] course & conversation very close, but could find no fault in him . . . I believed him to be a true man of God."

Tripp took Elder Kimball aside and looking him squarely in the eye, told him how he felt, that he was sincere in it, "but did not want to be deceived into any religious beliefs." Tripp earnestly scrutinized the church leader's face. "Elder Kimball then & there bore a faithful testimony that he was honest and sincere before God & that he knew Joseph Smith was a Prophet of God & that this was the true Church and Kingdom of God set up in the last days."

"I said to Mr. Kimball that if it was the work of God, to inform me. If it was the work of men, to so inform me."

Tripp said Kimball looked at him in earnest, his face white as snow, and declared: "Enoch, I see the integrity of thy heart and I say unto you in the name of the Lord, Jesus Christ, that this work is the work of God and not the work of man. . . . I promise you that if you will go forth into the waters of baptism, and have hands laid upon you for the gift of the Holy Ghost that you shall know for yourself that this is the work of God."

"I felt a shock go through me from the crown of my head to the soles of my feet, with the convincing power that it was the work of God. . . . I then had a witness of the truth of this latter-day work, and that testimony has always remained with me."

Tripp knew he could deny the truth no longer. He says, "I felt like it was my duty to be baptized." He was ready to make the greatest commitment of his life. But he had to act soon. The day neared (4 February 1846) when the Saints must leave their beloved Nauvoo. Once the exodus began, with its "Trail of Tears" across the Mississippi River, there would be little time for baptism.

The enemies of the Mormons were ever watchful to find and persecute Church leaders, so to avoid being conspicuous a large vessel was brought from the temple into the house and filled with water to conduct the baptismal ceremony of Tripp's relative with no "outsiders" looking in.

"I informed him [Kimball] that I was ready to go forward in baptism. I felt it was my duty to be baptized in the likeness of my death, burial & resurrection & a remission of my sins." Immediately following cousin Lyon's baptism, Tripp stepped into the water.

The next day, Tripp received his temple endowments, "the last night that they gave endowments in that [Nauvoo] temple."

Church leaders soon crossed over the Mississippi and were on their way west, "preparatory for a journey towards the Pacific Ocean." But having little money or means to travel, Tripp could not join them. Brother Kimball (as Tripp now refers to him) counseled Tripp to remain behind, to look after the lame, halt, blind, the aged, infirm, and the poor "for the mob would soon be upon them & they needed some young man with them." Kimball told Tripp he would be blessed if he would do so. Tripp affirmed that he would follow the church leader's instructions and join the others as soon as possible.

Brother Kimball seemed to be looking out for Tripp in yet another way. He suggested to Tripp that he and Roxana Sophia Billings, who had moved in to help Mrs. Lyon with her sewing, "might make a good match." Once the eternal skeptic of anything Mormon, Tripp took Kimball's advice a second time. Tripp and Sophia (as he called her) were married by Orson Hyde 29 March 1846. "We were only married then for time, after the manner of the Gentile world, for most of the heads of the church had left & there was no marrying for eternity." By this time most of those strong in the faith had departed.

The Saints remaining behind had to muster perhaps as much courage as the exiles facing west. The atrocities of Missouri were vivid reminders of what could happen for all who remained. Tripp was now among strangers, few friends, and little money. In the meantime, a hostile anti-Mormon mob was expected at almost any moment. Cannon fire was already pelting Nauvoo and had killed three of Tripp's friends, who he referred to as Brother Anderson, his son, and a Brother Norris.

Tripp dug in and began making a living for himself and his new bride by teaching school. At first, very few of the remaining church members, including Emma Smith, were willing to entrust this newcomer with their children. A month or so later, he was teaching so many students that Sophia had to help. Even Emma began sending her children to the Tripps' school. He and Sophia began to live more comfortably.

But mobs which had been holding back due to Mormon resistance, soon saw that fewer of that sect remained in the city; they grew bolder. Says Tripp's diary: "I was on duty day and night for nearly two weeks to defend our homes & families. I was in many close places, not knowing many times when I parted with my wife but what it would be the last time she would see me alive.

"A great many of the mob were killed but not ascertained how many; they always kept it very still." The mob, outnumbering the Mormons three to one, soon drove the Saints from their home "at the point of the bayonet . . . all the new citizens [who had come in to speculate] that took up arms had to leave too. They were called Jack Mormons."

(It would appear the term "Jack Mormon" did not at first mean a back-slider but a non-member living with Mormons, or someone thought by Church enemies to be in sympathy with Mormons.)

On or about 1 March 1847, Tripp and his wife "took a little bedding & clothing & fastened up the house with the balance of our things in it and took a steamboat for Burlington, Iowa." Not knowing who he could trust, Tripp "kept it dark that I was a Mormon." Later, "after things quieted down," he went back to Nauvoo in disguise to see what he could salvage from their old home, and managed to return to Burlington with a few items of furniture that remained.

The displaced Tripp now took up his father's old business as a shoe-maker and did well enough that he and Sophia could feel a small amount of economic security again. On 20 March 1847, Sophia gave birth to a son, naming him William after Tripp's father. They lived in Wapello, Iowa, for several years, prospering with hard work. But something was about to happen to Tripp and Sophia which would once again change his life.

In the fall of 1852, Tripp's cousin Peregrine Sessions, whom he had known in Nauvoo, stopped by to visit on his way to a mission to England. Tripp gave him ten dollars to help defray expenses and then sat back and listened as his cousin expounded on life in the Great Salt Lake Valley, the promised land of the Saints. Sessions reported to Tripp that "the Mormons were prospering first rate & . . . increasing very fast." Tripp was enthralled to learn how successfully his people had tamed the desert and "made it a good country."

One reason for the rapid growth of Zion was that polygamy was now being practiced openly. In fact, Parry had with him tracts written by Orson Pratt on the subject soon to be published and broadcast to all the world. Tripp sent Brother Pratt five dollars for him to send him two tracts, one for himself and one for his father in Maine.

The discussions with Sessions "had a tendency to strengthen me much in the faith as I have been here so long without seeing or hearing a Mormon talk." When Elder Sessions left for England, Tripp settled back to building a prosperous life for his wife and son, which seemed within reach.

But on 7 February 1853 (a date Tripp was never to forget) he was awakened about midnight by a voice repeating three times: "Get you up into the mountains." Thinking it might be his wife talking to him, Tripp turned over and woke her up but found she'd said nothing.

As Tripp lay on the bed, he was in deep misery. "In the anguish of my heart, I exclaimed that I would go & to close up my business & go to the valleys of the mountains." Sophia couldn't believe what her husband was saying. She did not share his idle dream to leave all they had built up with such diligent effort. Tripp shrugged; he must go alone. He would sell out his business, but first buy her a better home so that she could be more comfortably situated. He determined to do so, "the Lord being [his] helper."

Tripp said he felt calm as a summer's morning and lay back again. "In my sleep I saw the valley of Salt Lake & more particular, the southwest side of a mountain . . . " When he arrived in the Utah territory, he recognized the mountain as Ensign Peak. Instead of dust and sagebrush, he dreamed of beautiful houses, peach orchards, gardens, and green mountains surrounding the Great Salt Lake. All looked beautiful to him. Upon waking, he immediately placed an advertisement to raise money and go west.

As Tripp prepared for the long trek west, Sophia still refused to go with him. He bought four ox teams and two horse teams, and converted a wagon by adding a cook stove so that one could prepare meals in any weather and be comfortable. "It was a hard struggle for me to think of leaving her behind, for my love for her was great. She was a noble woman, a kind wife & affectionate mother to her children." Watching his energetic preparations, Sophia came to him and asked, "Are you determined to go & leave me & the children if we will not go with you?"

"I replied that I was . . . for in the Kingdom of God there is Eternal Life, Salvation & Exaltation & outside of it, Damnation"

She answered, "So long as you are determined to go, I will follow you, if I follow you to Hell."

Tripp and Sophia and their three sons departed for Zion on 3 April 1853, arriving 27 July. Horses were lost and other problems arose, but Tripp managed with courage, prayer, and hard work to overcome all his adversities. With the Lord's help, they would make it.

Upon nearing Zion, Tripp wrote: "we reached the summit of Big Mountain, which overlooks the Salt Lake Valley. Where the Saints dwell. My heart rejoiced within me as I cast my eyes over the valley. It seemed like emerging immediately from darkness into light . . . the valley looks beautiful." They then "drove the whole length of the valley" to his Aunt Sessions's home.

After spending about one year in Zion and building up a successful shoe repair business, Tripp received a mission call. It came on 27 June as the Saints held a special commemorative conference to honor Joseph Smith on the day he had been slain. The call caused some pondering in Tripp's heart. He and Sophia now had three sons and a comfortable life.

With his industrious habits, Tripp may have appeared more prosperous than he actually was. When Brother Kimball asked him for a loan of $200, Tripp writes, "I did not have enough money and told him so." Tripp even tried to borrow money from someone else to loan his friend who had helped him gain a testimony of the gospel. He was unable to do so.

When Tripp was soon thereafter called on the mission, rumors began to float about Zion that in denying Brother Kimball the loan of $200, Brother Kimball suddenly decided to send Tripp away for two years.

When Brother Kimball asked Tripp in a formal way if he intended on filling the mission call, Tripp responded, "Yes sir, by all means . . . so long as I am called by those that hold the authority over the Church and Kingdom of God upon the Earth . . . and not because I could not let you have the money."

Kimball did not mention the matter of money again but simply told Tripp, "You go and fill the mission & you shall be blessed & in him [Elder Kimball] I would always find a true friend."

Tripp replied that he always believed Elder Kimball to be a man of God and "had the best interest of the Kingdom of God at heart."

If Tripp had any serious question about whether he was called to serve by the Lord, he never mentioned it. Years later he was to write that President Brigham Young, in whom he had full confidence, gave him a departing blessing that if he did his part, the Lord would do his. "So far [at age seventy-two] every word promised me by Brigham Young has come to pass."

Elder Tripp was set apart for his mission by Apostle Orson Pratt, who blessed him he would travel in safety, that the Holy Ghost would open the way and strengthen his understanding. Tripp and Sophia also received patriarchal blessings at this time. Tripp was told he would prosper upon the Earth and be entitled to all the blessings of Tripp of old, that he "would walk with the Lord upon the Earth and live until I was satisfied with life."

Tripp sold his shoe repair business and procured mules and mountain ponies as advised, to fulfil his mission to Texas. He departed 4 September, camping out the first night in Emigration Canyon with other missionaries heading east, including mission president John Taylor. But before going to his assigned field in Texas, he obtained permission to visit his parents in Maine. En route there he visited old acquaintances in Iowa. Some, upon finding he was a Mormon, were "perfectly raving" against him, calling Joseph Smith names and saying that "the Government ought to send up an army & wipe that people out."

Talking to a man from Quincy, Illinois, Tripp was told that "Nauvoo is going down fast & is a great harbor for thieves and robbers & that the widow of the prophet Joseph Smith had married a Gentile by the name of 'Badamon' & that she had lost the spirit of Mormonism & also all her children." Tripp seemed greatly saddened that Emma, the noble help-meet of the Prophet Joseph through so many hardships, had left the true Church.

Tripp also met with his wife's sister, by now a member. Her husband was not; "they were very unhappy together."

When he arrived in Ripley, Maine, Tripp's parents flung their arms around him. It had been nine years. His younger brothers and sisters "had grown out of my knowledge." He stayed up to a late hour answering all their questions. His father was now a Freewill Baptist preacher, "leaving the Methodist faith because there were more Baptists about now and they desired him to join with them. He did so, thinking he would feel more at home with them. My father is one of the most honorable men on the Earth . . . but he is blinded by the priest craft of the day."

Tripp bore strong testimony of the restored Church to his family, telling all that had befallen him, even speaking to his father's congregation for over an hour. But prejudice against "outside" faiths was strong; Tripp wrote of a Methodist priest speaking strongly against the Catholic Church and "said with much warmth that the Catholick [sic] Church ought to be exterminated." Tripp adds: "In a small town of Ellsworth not far from here they tarred and feathered and rode on a rail a Catholic priest out of town."

But this didn't stop the Mormon missionary from preaching to his family and the local Penobscot Indian Tribe. "We called at the chief's house. He wasn't home. We then called on his delegate who represents them in the State Legislature. I bore my testimony to him of the true gospel of Christ and that my people have the record of their forefathers, which he seemed much interested in."

Tripp gives no further details about his visit to the Penobscot Indians but concludes: "I feel that when the full times come for the Gospel to be turned to the House of Israel that this People will readily receive it."

None of Tripp's family would join him in his new church. "They all look upon me as being deluded & as the scripture says, they have ears and hear not, & eyes & see not & hearts and understand not the things of God."

After Tripp had been repeatedly rebuffed in several villages near his hometown, he decided to "cast pearls among swine no longer." He bid them farewell and set out into the countryside to find others desirous to learn about the restored Church. Tripp was realistic in his missionary endeavors, telling potential converts that "If you come here [Zion] you must make up your mind to go through many privations and be persecuted on every hand, for so they persecuted the saints in Jesus's day, and so long as we are not of the world, the world will hate us."

Tripp baptized and confirmed fifteen members in Maine "and set several old members on the right track again." When his mission president found out about Elder Tripp's success, Tripp's request for a change was granted that he might serve the remainder of his mission in Maine rather than going to Texas. As had Elder Wilford Woodruff years before, Elder Tripp visited a number of communities in New England and preached with great energy and vitality to all who would listen. A number of souls were baptized.

On his way home after serving a faithful mission, Tripp visited with old friends in Nauvoo. As he walked the streets, memories surrounded him. He reminisced that Nauvoo, the place the Mormons had built a flourishing city, now "looks like a mass of ruins. The temple which stood upon a hill, built of white polished lime rock, and could be seen for scores of miles, and was the largest and most beautiful building in the whole great West . . . the front walls are all that remain. I received my endowments in it, being on the night of the 2nd of February, 1846, being the last night that the servants of God worked in the House before having to take their flight . . . to flee from the hands of their enemies that were already seeking their lives. Oh! how changed. The wicked can soon destroy what will take the saints of God years in their poor and half-starved condition to build up. Now, I must turn my eyes from this once lovely city."

Enoch Bartlett Tripp was one of those referred to by President Gordon B. Hinckley on 27 June 2002 during the dedication of the Nauvoo Temple, as a pioneer whose life and heart was tied to the house of the Lord, and who was "surely present now" to see it rebuilt in all its former magnificence.

Tripp noted that the bodies of Joseph and Hyrum "lay sleeping beneath the Bee Stand near the Prophet's mansion where his widow and mother now live." Tripp reasoned that their spirits would be teaching in spirit prison as taught in 1 Peter 3:18.

"I called on the prophet's widow, children and mother. All were pleased to see me. The children were once my pupils, when I taught school in the city before I was driven from it with the rest of the saints."

Tripp found Emma totally removed both emotionally and spiritually from the Utah Mormons. "She was very bitter against President Brigham Young and his followers & never desires to gather up, and all of her children partake of the same spirit." Tripp describes the eldest son, Joseph, as a man purporting to be a spiritual medium who could communicate with his father by placing hands on pencil and paper. Tripp explained to him that he was being deceived, that that was not of God. "I warned him against this great evil and to turn and walk in the narrow path his Father has laid out through Christ . . . for all men to walk in."

He then called on Lucy Mack, whom Emma had been caring for in her old age. It was apparently one of the last interviews ever held with the grand lady of the Church. "I called on the Prophet's mother and found her in bed in a lonely room on the east part of the house and very feeble. Upon approaching her bedside and informing her who I was, she arose in her bed and placing her arms around my neck, kissed me, exclaiming, "I can now die in peace since I have beheld your face from the valleys of the mountains."

Lucy "made inquiries after the Saints and remarked that she took much comfort in riding [in the country] with me and my wife in the day that I taught school here. But all those days and happy scenes are past and her day is near at hand when she must bid adieu to this earth and meet with her loves ones beyond the veil."

Open and warm, she recalled many happy memories, and told Tripp to take her love to church leaders in Zion.

He concludes, "I received a farewell blessing from a great mother in Israel."

This latter report by Tripp does much to let today's Saints know that Emma truly cared about her mother-in-law as she took care of her to her dying day. It also lets us know about Lucy's continued love for the "Utah Church" even though none of her immediate family went west with Brigham Young.

Tripp returned to Utah to live with great devotion to the church which he had been warned to only associate with at peril of his life. Relatives now meet often to give thanks that he traveled to Nauvoo to find out for himself if stories told about the Church by its enemies were true.

EPILOGUE

Enoch Bartlett Tripp, the man who "wanted nothing to do with the Mormon religion," continued to do missionary work until his death 25 January 1909. Before Tripp's death, his father in Maine told him he knew the gospel his son preached to be true—and that if he lived long enough, he would join his son in Zion. "As father did not live long enough to come to Utah, I had my parents' work done in the temple."

Tripp had five wives, Roxana Sophia Billings, Phoebe Peterson, Jessie Smith Eddings, Kate Jane Allen, and Mary Openshaw. Altogether Tripp was blessed with thirty-two children and sixty-five grandchildren.

Guiding the final years of Tripp's life was a patriarchal blessing given in 1871 which said: "The Lord knowest thy integrity. . . . Thy name shall be handed down with thy Posterity in honorable remembrance from Generation to Generation."

It was, of course, made possible by the life this pioneer convert led. He was truly a stalwart through many storms throughout his life, and we are blessed that he kept such meticulous records that others might benefit from his experiences.

NOTES

Tripp, E. B. Personal journals and diaries, Volumes 1–18 in transcript. Brigham Young University Lee Library Special Collections, Provo, Utah. Also, Tripp's Overview, as noted. All are in possession of author.

Tripp, George C. Personal journal. Compiled by Gladys Tripp; in possession of author.

(Statements by Tripp can be corroborated, so far as official history is known, by cross-referencing with B.H. Roberts in *History of the Church*, as noted.)

Chapter 2: Justice

ALEXANDER DONIPHAN
and LYMAN WIGHT

"It is cold-blooded murder. I will not obey your order."

It is an incredible experience to see the large monument in the public square at Richmond, Missouri, dedicated to Brigadier General Alexander Doniphan. Wasn't he the one who defied the whole state of Missouri, including its governor in 1838, by refusing to execute Joseph Smith, the Mormon prophet, the most hated man in the state? And wasn't it a direct order from a superior military officer for which Doniphan himself could have been court-martialed and executed, but never was?

Yes, it was Alexander Doniphan who uttered the memorable words that courageously defended the Latter-day Saints in one of their darkest hours: "It is cold-blooded murder. I will not obey your order. . . . And if you execute these men, I will hold you responsible before an earthly tribunal, so help me God."

Doniphan simply and boldly walked away from the order. But he did even more—he daily risked his life and career by standing up for the Mormon leaders, even after a decree of extermination had been issued by Missouri Governor Lilburn Boggs. That decree stated that not only should the Mormons be driven from the state but intercepted and exterminated before they might escape to Illinois.

Latter-day Saint Lyman Wight, in an affidavit filed before the Missouri courts, had this to say about the execution which was to take place at 8 A.M., 1 November 1838: "At the removal of Gen. Doniphan's part of the army, the camp was thrown into the utmost confusion and consternation. Gen. [Samuel] Lucas, fearing the consequences of such hasty and inconsiderate measures, revoked the decree of shooting the prisoners." For the time being, the lives of the Mormon leaders were saved.

Probably no greater courage than Doniphan's was ever recorded in military history. Yet, in Doniphan's autobiography, he didn't even mention Joseph Smith or the "Mormon War"! Nor did he in any of his surviving letters. True, he considered Joseph Smith a good man, but a prophet of God? Those who knew Doniphan said he belonged to no church. He was at the time considered an atheist.

Why then such an act of flagrant disobedience for someone with whom he didn't even agree philosophically? There could be many answers, but the one which stands out above all the others is that Alexander William Doniphan carried such a strong sense of justice and fair play for all men under the Constitution—including even an unpopular man such as Joseph Smith—that his peers feared to oppose him. How this conviction came about is the story of a remarkable man.

To paint a physical portrait of Alexander, he stood six feet four inches tall and carried an impressive physique, with deep-set eyes and a prominent chin. (One biographer went so far as to say Alexander "possessed a manly beauty Greek sculptors would love to copy.") Even more impressive perhaps was his mental "physique." Doniphan's boyhood hero was lawyer and legislator Henry Clay. The latter's oratory held Congress spellbound as he sought to resolve differences between slave and non-slave holders. While Doniphan may have held no illusions in swaying audiences as did Clay, Doniphan sought to match Clay's wisdom and achievements as much as possible.

Doniphan's wisdom rang eloquently, albeit sometimes ignored, throughout Missouri. It fell on the deaf ears of Missouri's Judge A. A. King. Told by the Mormons that yes, they believed in the seventh chapter of Daniel (a kingdom of God to come forth in the latter days), King turned to the clerk and said, "Write that down; it is a strong mark for treason."

Doniphan's reply: "Judge, you had better make the Bible treason."

When the defendants were told to bring in witnesses who might speak in their behalf, any who did evoked great hostility in the courtroom. Any witness for the defense was thrown out, often barely escaping with his life. Ascertaining the prejudice running rampant, Doniphan wisely advised the Mormons to call no more witnesses. Said he, "Though a legion of angels from the opening heavens should declare your innocence, the court and populace have decreed your destruction."

There were many reasons, of course, why the backwoods Missourians brooked no sympathy for the Saints, which sentiment had even extended to the elected politicians and judges. One was the Mormon's perceived holier-than-thou religious views; another was that their increased numbers could influence the vote; another was they came mostly from New England and were considered abolitionists. Church leaders had never announced such a position, but the mobsters were in no mood to sit down and discuss fine political points with "foreigners." Additionally, it was known that the Book of Mormon was sympathetic to the Native Americans and the Missourians feared return of Indians to their borders. Were the Mormons in collaboration with the natives? For the mob element, few of them well educated and highly suspicious of outsiders, it was simple: get rid of this potential threat to their way of life.

While the Mormons had few friends during this trying period, several Missouri generals witnessed the injustices being done against them and initially tried to turn back the angry rabble. But none did so as eloquently and effectively as Doniphan. General David Atchison, convinced that the Saints were being unfairly treated, wrote the governor to that effect. Boggs promptly removed him from the campaign against the "insurgents," even though Atchison had seniority over the general who replaced him. Doniphan, who resisted even more strenuously, was never removed.

General H. G. Parks also sided with the Mormons when he beheld the injustices done to them by Missouri mobs. But in the face of a growing rabble, Parks lacked the courage of Doniphan to help the downtrodden Saints.

The Mormons did not have to deal with an organized militia in New York or Ohio, as they did in Missouri. That made things worse, for when they were driven from their Missouri homes at gunpoint, Mormons could not call on the law for assistance. Militia-directed mobs were the law.

The Mormons faced their fiercest opposition from four Missouri officers: Generals Wilson (no first name given by Smith's *History of the Church*), Lucas, John B. Clark, and the particularly treacherous Colonel George Hinkle. Hinckle promised a truce, but when the Saints gave up their arms under a white flag agreement, Hinckle delivered them up to be arrested.

Church member Lyman Wight, who had lived in Missouri long enough (actually near present Adam-ondi-Ahman) to be included in the Missouri militia, refused to bear arms against the Mormon leader. General Wilson curtly told Wight, "We do not wish to hurt you . . . but we have one thing against you . . . you are too friendly to Joe Smith."

When asked to "swear all you know about him," Wight answered, "I then told Wilson that I believed said Smith to be the most philanthropic man I ever saw . . . a friend to mankind, a maker of peace . . . and sir, had it not been that I had given heed to his counsel, I would have given you hell before this time and all your mob forces."

This did not sit well with the general. "Wight, I fear your life is in danger, for there is no end to the prejudice against Joe Smith." (Note there was no mention of evidence, or official charges.) Wilson summed it up: "I regret to tell you your die is cast; your doom is fixed; you are to be shot tomorrow morning on the public square at Far West, at eight o' clock."

Said Wight: "Shoot and be damned."

It was not meant as a curse; Wight appeared to mean what he said literally. General Wilson would be damned if he harmed a prophet of the Lord. Lyman had such a sincere love for the Prophet that he was willing to die at his side.

Wight was to be executed along with Joseph and Hyrum Smith, Parley Parker Pratt, Sidney Rigdon, Amasa Lyman, and George Robinson. Labeled "Wild Ram of the Mountains" by one biographer, Wight joined the Mormon cause with members of Sidney Rigdon's Campbellite flock in Kirtland, Ohio. With other Rigdonites, he "had all things in common." After joining the new church, Wight went wherever his fierce loyalty to the Mormon prophet took him. In Cincinnati, a zealous Elder Wight baptized over a hundred souls.

Lyman sheds much light on Alexander Doniphan's thoughts about being ordered to execute Smith. Knowing Wight's admiration for Joseph, Doniphan confided to Wight (*History of the Church* 3:437–449) that his superiors' order to kill the Mormon leader was "a damned hard one. I have washed my hands against such cool and deliberate murder."

After Doniphan shocked his military leaders by announcing his refusal to shoot Joseph, General Lucas wasn't yet finished. He showed his barbaric bias against the Latter-day Saint leaders by exhibiting them for public ridicule in the town square at Far West. This was a singular outrage, for Far West was the heart of Caldwell County, the same one that had been legislated (Doniphan being a factor in the Missouri legislature) for peaceful Mormon settlement. Doniphan's efforts went for naught in this instance, because rather than solving the "Mormon problem," Missouri citizenry soon coveted even the treeless and seemingly barren lands of Caldwell County. By driving the newcomers away, their industry was up for grabs.

Joseph and the other Mormon leaders were routed through the Richmond Jail where General Clark again tried to have them shot. But "doubtful of his authority," and remembering the stern rebuke by General Doniphan, Clark sent to Fort Leavenworth for military advice, according to Wight. He tells us that cooler heads prevailed among U.S. military officials. Lucas "was informed that any such proceedings would be cold-blooded and heartless murder."

Nevertheless, Clark charged his prisoners with "treason, murder, arson, burglary, larceny, theft and stealing and various other charges too tedious to mention at this time." Soon afterward, Judge King made the unnecessary statement that there "would be no law for the Mormons and they needn't expect any." Further, he told his prisoners that if Governor Boggs's extermination order had been directed to him, "it would have been fulfilled ere this time."

Joseph and the others were then moved to Liberty Jail. Once the state grew embarrassed in holding the Mormon leaders without cause, though, they were allowed to escape. Interestingly, while Doniphan suffered no popular outcry from the Missouri mobs, nor any mutiny from his soldiers in assisting the Mormon prophet while chastising superiors, the jailers who "let" Joseph and company escape from Liberty Jail, were bullied and beaten. According to *History of the Church* 3:321, the mob dragged one jailer by the hair of his head across the town square.

Doniphan's threat to hold those responsible for the prophet's death "before an earthly tribunal, so help me God!" was not an idle threat. He attempted repeatedly to defend the Mormons in court. And Doniphan was known as a most able lawyer. In the hundred and eight cases where he acted as counsel over a period of thirty years, no defendants of his were ever convicted of the maximum charges against them. He was known as a man with determination and influence "who held the oratory power to sway juries."

He also became a Christian. A Baptist newsletter, published by William Jewell College, Liberty, Missouri, honors Doniphan "for keeping his word in riding horseback in all weather" to raise funds for their college. As for the "charge" of being an atheist, it was removed after Doniphan joined the local Christian Church. (This occurred after Alexander suffered severe personal tragedy. Death took his only two sons, and for years before her death, Doniphan nursed an ailing wife he dearly loved.) The William Jewell College Bulletin says that Doniphan's baptism left many people "cheering that he had formally ended his atheism."

One relationship that had a strong influence on his life was a mother who encouraged him "to seek truth from the best books and to inculcate habits of honesty and industry." He was an avid student from a young age. Born 9 July 1808, Alexander entered Augusta College at age fourteen, graduating four years later with distinction. After two more years' study, he passed the bar and moved to what appeared to be a land wide open with opportunity for the practice of law: Liberty, Clay County, Missouri.

The unschooled border ruffians of Missouri who rebelled against their own state constitution (which proclaimed religious tolerance for all, as did many local Protestant churches) clearly went against Doniphan's sense of justice and fair play. Missouri's mobsters flouted the law, as they put it, "because the evil is one that no one could have foreseen and is therefore, unprovided for in the laws."

But Doniphan had sworn as a lawyer to uphold the Missouri Constitution, even Article XIII, Section Four, which reads: "That all men have a natural and indefensible right to worship Almighty God according to the dictates of their own conscience . . . that no human authority can control or interfere with the rights of conscience; that no person can ever be hurt, molested, or restrained in his religious persuasion."

A sham was being perpetrated before the astute Missouri lawyer's eyes. He fought it with all his soul.

As a new attorney, Doniphan had his first contact with the Mormon leaders when Joseph Smith hired him and his three partners in law to help extract them from legal difficulties with Missouri sheriffs. The price to defend them was $250 per attorney. The firm allowed this was a lofty price, but explained that prejudice ran heavily against these would-be clients; if the attorneys took up for the Mormons, they were sure to lose other business, almost certainly a correct assumption.

However, Doniphan confided to Joseph that his firm would like to represent the Saints because the mob element had tried to threaten them not to do so. As professionals, they were not about to buckle under frontier pressure. "We wish to show them we disregard their empty bravado." Doniphan was willing, perhaps eager, to take up for the underdog.

Joseph Smith must have admired the legal skills of his hired counsel, for he wrote in his history, "President Rigdon and myself commenced this day to study law, under the direction of Generals Atchison and Doniphan. They think by diligent application, we can be admitted to the bar in twelve months."

Hiring Doniphan and Atchison was, in fact, the only legal recourse the churchmen had at the time. Doniphan went to work quickly in confronting the military courts. Said he, "A court martial would be illegal as hell. Civilians are not subject to military law." (Doniphan is oft quoted as punctuating his remarks with swear words. It might have been the only language some Missourians understood.)

In a public meeting where Doniphan acted not as a lawyer but only as a private citizen, he told those gathered that he "admired the Mormons for trying to protect their fellow church members. . . . Unless the saints were cowards, they should be allowed to keep their arms to protect themselves . . . Greater love can no man show than he who lays down his life for his brethren."

Doniphan was clearly impressed early with the Mormon leaders and their attitude in the face of adversity. He described them as "peaceable, sober, industrious, a law-abiding people. . . . I have never met a group of men who had the native intelligence and understanding and force of character that have ever quite equaled the group of leaders gathered about Joseph Smith."

Atchison did not describe them at such length but when ordered to strike against the "insurgents," he wrote Governor Boggs: "I have no doubt your excellency has been deceived by the exaggerated statements of designing or half crazy men. I have found there is no cause for alarm on account of the Mormons; they are not to be feared; they are very much alarmed. . . . I do not feel to disgrace myself or permit the troops under my command to disgrace themselves by acting the part of a mob. If the Mormons are to be driven from their homes, let it be done without any color of law and in open defiance thereof."

So why was Atchison replaced and not Doniphan? Perhaps Doniphan was simply savvy enough to not vent his feelings to the governor in writing, and by so doing, avoided the governor's wrath. There is another possibility, however; Atchison at one time wavered on his defense of the Saints. On 28 December 1838, he wrote Governor Boggs that the Mormons "have set the laws of the country at defiance." It was the only time Atchison ever wavered on the Mormon issue, but it may have been enough to signal a weakness in resolution on the matter. In contrast, it would seem that because of Doniphan's never-flailing courage, no man in Missouri or elsewhere dared to defy or confront him. Doniphan's motto seemed to be, "Believe in something strong enough to back it up with grit—whatever the consequence."

Even years later, in command of a volunteer Missouri army fighting against Mexico in Santa Fe, Doniphan praised the arriving Mormon Battalion. Doniphan's biographer, Gregory Maynard, said the general took it upon himself to order a hundred-gun salute fired in "honor of the Mormons' loyalty to the country, despite the wrongs they had suffered."

Volunteering to enter the fray against Mexico as a private, Doniphan's bent for leadership soon found him elected to the rank of colonel. He attained military distinction by taking his rag-tag "farm boy" regiment of 924 U.S. Missouri patriots behind enemy lines. Just eighteen miles south of Chihuahua, living off the land and minus any reinforcements, Doniphan's regiment defeated two Mexican armies, said to number 4,120. The "Show Me" state's volunteers had shown the world their backwoods determination. And when the incident resulted in much of central Mexico coming under U.S. control, Doniphan found himself a war hero.

And he wasn't through. When the Civil War reared its ugly head, he addressed 6,000 of his fellow citizens, standing in the cold, to persuade them to remain loyal to the Union. Many were slave-holders and had strong Confederate leanings. Henry Clay himself might have been no more eloquent.

An admitted slave holder along with his peers, Doniphan nevertheless was willing to give them up, on principle, to avoid dividing his country.

President Abraham Lincoln was impressed. Missouri had tried to give Doniphan a Confederate commission but he declined. Single-handedly almost, that act seemed to change the state's affections for secession to loyalty for President Lincoln. Doniphan's courageous action in behalf of the

American flag did not escape the president's notice. It brought a personal audience with "Honest Abe" in Washington D. C. Modestly, Doniphan does not record what the president said to him.

The Jewell College Bulletin summed it up: Doniphan was "honest and modest to the extreme, scorning hypocrisy and sham, a symbol of pioneer Americanism." And the Baptist bulletin stated this about General Doniphan's action in helping the Mormon cause: "To this day, the Mormons consider Col. Doniphan the greatest Gentile who ever lived."

When visiting Salt Lake City in 1874, Doniphan received a warm welcome. The general who had befriended the Mormons at perhaps their lowest point in history made no speeches claiming honor for his deed. He would do the same for anyone. Doniphan, even though he wasn't a member, was nevertheless a most revered man. It was this that led to his admirers erecting a memorial to this "noble man" in Richmond, Missouri. Doniphan had transcended both Missouri and Mormon differences, while maintaining and defending his principles. Now, both placed him on a pedestal. Most importantly, Doniphan's innate sense of justice kept him from placing any goal he might have had for being a lawyer, statesman, or general, above being first a man of integrity and a champion for justice.

NOTES

Duchateau, Andre. *Missouri Colossus*. Stillwater: Oklahoma St. University Press, 1973.

Maynard, Gregory, "Alexander William Doniphan: Man of Justice, " *BYU Studies*, Summer 1973, 13:4, 472.

Maynard, Gregory, *Alexander Doniphan Lawyer, Educator, Statesman and Soldier*. Provo: Brigham Young University Press, 1972.

Pratt, Parley Parker. *Autobiography*, Salt Lake City, Utah: Deseret Book, 1961.

Smith, Joseph, *History of the Church*, Vol. 1–3, Salt Lake City, Utah: Deseret Book, 1980.

Wight, Jermy. 'Wild Ram of the Mountain," *Star Valley Llama*, Bedford, Wyoming, 1996.

Wight, Jermy. Telephone interview. Bedford, Wyoming. 21 January 2000.

Wight, Lyman, "An Address, Journal of my Life," Austin: Wight Trust Publishers, Spring, 1848.

William Jewell College Bulletin: "Col. Doniphan, Symbol of Pioneer Americanism," Liberty, Missouri., 20:7, 1947. Alumni address: Settle, Raymond.

Wixom, Hartt, *Edward Partridge, First Bishop of the Church*, Springville: Cedar Fort, 1998.

World Book Encyclopedia. Chicago: Field Enterprises, Vol. 4., 1968.

Chapter 3: Faith

SYLVESTER HENRY EARL

"Earl plunged into his work with renewed zeal."

The young Mormon elder was in trouble and he knew it. He had just finished a sermon in the back country of Illinois about the heavens being opened and the Lord restoring His true church to the earth. "Did anyone want to be baptized?" The baptismal service would begin at 4 P.M.

A young lady, twenty years of age, rose up and walked forward. She was the only one in the audience to do so. In the words of a family member, the action "surprised the congregation, astonished her parents and enraged her brothers." They talked about returning with guns.

As the hour approached, the girl's parents attempted in vain to talk her out of joining this "strange new cult." The three brothers took their guns off the wall and loaded them. They persuaded three cousins to bring their guns. No Mormon was going to baptize their sister! The six of them would teach this Elder Earl a lesson he would never forget!

Confused and lonely, Lois Caroline Owen left the others to find a quiet place where she might pray. After so doing, she was more convinced than ever that she should join this new church. When she headed for the water's edge, parents, brothers, and cousins followed with determination to stop the proceedings.

Elder Sylvester Henry Earl invited the assembled crowd to sing a song: "The clouds of error disappear / Before the rays of truth divine; . . . / The glory bursting from afar / Wide o'er the nations soon will shine" ("The Morning Breaks," *Hymn* #1).

Stepping upon a log to speak, the elder tried not to look at the six angry men before him, leaning forward to catch every word, guns cocked. Yet, he couldn't help seeing them from the corner of his eyes.

Clearly, what he said here and now might determine whether a new spirit entered the Lord's Kingdom—and whether he lived another day. It was no time to be timid. The young missionary had to muster his courage. He said a silent prayer and summoned his vocal chords.

For three quarters of an hour, Elder Earl addressed the assemblage. He assured them the Lord had again spoken from the heavens. The more he spoke, the more he felt imbued with a power from on high. He told the audience before him that God had raised up a modern-day prophet named Joseph Smith and given him the authority to act in His name . . . and that through him the everlasting gospel would be restored. The Zion spoken of in the Old Testament would be gathered once again. All in the audience might gain their salvation and prepare to meet their Savior at the Second Coming if baptized into this new church.

Then the elder stepped down. Not a word was spoken by the congregation. All seemed as if spellbound. Or was it anger and disbelief?

Elder Earl took the young woman by the hand, led her into the nearby stream, and baptized her in the name of the Father, the Son, and the Holy Ghost. When they came up out of the water, Lois was confirmed a member of The Church of Jesus Christ of Latter-day Saints. The six men with cocked guns did not move a muscle, other than to bow their heads.

Lois's family told her that while they did not approve of her action, she was welcome to her beliefs and could remain at home. Earl departed Schuyler County, Illinois, for a time, and then returned to visit the young woman who had braved the storm of opposition. He found her sister, Betsy Ann, also interested in the new faith. The family treated the missionary warmly by now, the brothers raising no opposition.

After concluding his missionary work in western Illinois, Sylvester Earl returned to marry Lois Caroline Owen, first civilly, later for time and eternity.

The story of Sylvester Henry Earl and Lois Caroline Owen is preserved by family records, starting with the unpublished journal of Sylvester himself. They are a testament to the keeping of personal histories. Without their journals, the story of how these two met and fell in love because of their faith in the restored gospel might have been lost forever.

Earl was twenty-one years old when he had first heard of the restored gospel. He was not a tall man, as he described himself, about five feet seven inches in height and of dark complexion. But he walked with a quick, energetic step and embraced the gospel with similar enthusiasm. After being baptized by Apostle Charles C. Rich, Earl traveled in the summer of 1837 to Far West, Missouri. Here he found himself in the middle of a terrible and devastating war between his adopted people, the Mormons, and suspicious, backwoods Missourians. The Mormons were charged with claiming to commune with angels, and perceived as believing only they would be saved. They were also from New England, and therefore they had to be abolitionists. To uneducated "border ruffians," their traditional way of life was being threatened; they must unite "to eliminate the Mormon menace." For Elder Earl, it was a severe test of his new faith. The devil could not have devised one more difficult.

After buying ninety acres of land near Far West, a yoke of oxen, and several cows, and after clearing the land and starting to build a home, he was called by local leaders to go on a mission to Illinois, Indiana, and Ohio. He faced a new and different challenge, for he had almost no education and possessed little knowledge of the scriptures or any confidence in preaching it. All he had was his faith. He would need a lot of it.

He grew so discouraged with his abilities that when he met Joseph Smith and his family coming in from Kirtland, Earl sank down on a log and pleaded for a blessing. Joseph promised him that if he would be prayerful, his tongue would be loosed, that the Bible would no longer be a sealed book but be open to him . . . and that he would bring many souls to a knowledge of the truth. Elder Earl was also told that he should not be confounded, nor suffer harm. With a parting "God bless you" from the Prophet, the new missionary "went away rejoicing."

Earl plunged into his work with renewed faith in himself and his work, almost immediately finding success. He helped organize branches and leadership to guide them. Family records say his "heart was set upon the great latter-day work, a fisher and hunter of souls according to the words of Jeremiah." He soon persuaded his brothers, Joseph Wilbur and James Calvin, to join him as they proselyted through Illinois to Schuyler County where Sylvester met and baptized Lois Caroline.

After the two were married, the couple moved to Hancock County, Illinos, near Nauvoo. When persecution began to mount, Earl moved into Nauvoo itself, thinking there would be greater safety in numbers.

Not necessarily so. He was constantly embroiled in defending the city. As an experienced horseman, he was out night and day carrying express messages from leaders to members. He nearly lost his life several times to marauding mobs but managed each time to escape.

He was also a member of the Nauvoo Legion and remembered well the Prophet's "memorable" speech to the Mormon militia on 18 June 1844. This address, the last Joseph made to his men, was in full uniform on the top of a building frame where he could see every man and they him. The last words of his one-and-a-half-hour speech, as reported by Earl, were these: "I do not regard my own life. I am ready to be offered a sacrifice for this people; for what can our enemies do? Only kill the body and their power is at an end. Stand firm, my friends. Never flinch."

He told the large crowd assembled that they should become like Gods if they remained faithful. "God has tried you. You are a good people; therefore, I love you with all my heart. Greater love hath no man than that he should lay down his life for his friends. You have stood by me in the hour of trouble, and I am willing to sacrifice my life for your preservation."

One wonders if Emma fully realized what Joseph was saying, that he sensed his impending death. There was no other way, it seemed, but to seal his testimony with his blood. The effect upon young Sylvester was to rededicate his life to serve his faith more resolutely: He worked on the Nauvoo Temple, guarding it often night and day against an expected wave of invading rabble. He felt a deep kinship with his Maker, he wrote, during these perilous times. He and Lois received their endowments in the temple early in 1845, shortly before it fell into hands of the enemy.

After Joseph's death, Earl's eyewitness history includes the well-known appearance of Sidney Rigdon as "guardian" of the church, and also the speech of Brigham Young. "Attention, all Israel," Young began. Earl said President Young's countenance was transformed into the likeness of Joseph. "All doubts vanished. They knew him to be the true Shepherd of Latter-day Israel. They were as ready to follow President Young as they had been Joseph."

Sylvester and Lois left Nauvoo 10 February 1846. While those who departed 4 February were able to cross on the ice, the Earls along with many other Saints floated across the Mississippi in flatboats. Earl wrote that men with nail-studded poles remained vigilant on the upstream side to push away random ice floes. Boats ran day and night for weeks.

Upon arrival in Council Bluffs, the Earls spent the remainder of the year helping build homes and furniture in Council Bluffs. Earl proved to be a natural carpenter.

In the spring, Earl, now thirty-one, was selected to go west with the first company of 149 pioneers (144 men, three women, and two children). He writes, "It is hard to leave my family here, sick and among the howling wolves and roaming savages . . . but the servants of the Lord say go." (His remarks are recorded in *111 Days to Zion, The Day by Day Trek of the Mormon Pioneers*, 7.)

Elder Earl traveled in the company of ten captained by Stephen Goddard which arrived in Great Salt Lake Valley on 23 July 1847. So little was said of Sylvester during the journey in *111 Days to Zion* that either he did not spend a great deal of time in the presence of camp historian William Clayton (Earl's group included none of the twelve apostles), or apparently he did not get in any noticeable trouble along the way.

Returning for his family in the spring of 1848, Earl had almost no money. To make do, he traded the shirt off his back to Indians for dried buffalo meat which he rationed among his family. He then cut up part of the wagon cover to make a new shirt.

One of the Earl children, Hyrum, died in Council Bluffs and another, Sylvester Jr., was born en route west. In the Great Salt Lake Valley, Earl became recognized as a master mechanic, fixing tools, plows, harrows, wagons, and making household furniture. He made a spinning wheel used by the family, as well as the reel and loom on which Lois utilized raw wool and cotton to make clothing for the family. He later also served a mission to England. All else had to be put aside in 1857 when he was called on for a short period to help keep Johnston's Army out of Zion.

In 1861, he was called by President Young to help settle Pine Valley in the Dixie Country. One reason was that President Young knew that Earl, with his turning lathe, could make all kinds of furniture, including spinning wheels and looms for the new frontier community. Thus, Earl brought the first lathe to the lumbering camps at Pine Valley and was likely the first cabinet maker in the county.

In those days, Pine Valley was emerging into a cattle town in that cowboys wintering their herds farther south (Santa Clara and Beaverdam Wash) stopped in to let cattle fatten before the long drive to the railroad at Modena near the Nevada border. The latter was, in effect, a Great Basin version of Dodge City, Kansas. Whether Earl took up with any of the cattle drives is not known, but it did add a Wild West atmosphere to a town already on the edge of the western frontier. Some fans of Zane Grey even think the author writing his novels of the Southwest in the early 1900s might have been thinking of Pine Valley.

By now, Sylvester had taken a second wife, Margaret Emily Jones, an English convert who would bear him three children. He arrived in Pine Valley on upper Santa Clara Creek on a cold 25 November and put his family in a large tent that had been brought in by Johnston's Army to Salt Lake Valley in 1857. A fire was built in it every night where the women did the cooking; smoke vented through a two-foot wide hole in the roof. The children later reported the experience as a "wonderful camping trip." Other families came over for the evening, played music, or sang songs. The children wrote in their journals that these were days of pleasant memories. They also wrote that they grew to love Sylvester dearly for the time he was willing to spend with them.

Later, because of troubles with the local Indians (mostly Piutes, although Navajos raided occasionally to steal horses), Sylvester moved his families to St. George. Life was easier there; the lower elevation winters were not as cold and bleak as in Pine Valley. It was here as a parent that Sylvester was to face one of the most trying decisions of his life. Whether it was the right one or not depends upon one's point of view.

A nineteen-year-old Mormon youth by the name of Solomon Avery Wixom, heading south from Salt Lake City with friends toward the California gold fields, stopped in St. George. He had grown bored in the city of the Saints and succumbed to the siren song of his gold-seeking peers. They had convinced him there was easy money and adventure just several days' journey away.

But in reaching Utah's Dixie, the group decided they needed more supplies; they would have to earn extra money before continuing on. Sol, as most who knew him called him, was a social sort, striking up a conversation easily with the older Sylvester Henry Earl. The affable lad reminded Earl of the son he had lost crossing the plains. Somewhat footloose, Sol seemed to need a father to look after him.

Going to the gold fields, was he? "Why don't you come home and have dinner with us. We can talk this thing over."

The boy learned that Earl had joined the church in Ohio, where his own family traveled after being baptized in New York. Sylvester offered the boy a job in St. George. Sol felt tempted by the gold fields and the urging of his friends, but one thing made him decide to stay: the Earl's auburn-haired daughter, Lois Orenia, who had been named after her mother. Sol wrote in his journals that she "was the most beautiful creature I had ever seen."

What did she think of him? He was a hard worker. He had studied math, shorthand, and gained skills which could lead to a future in the upcoming field of telegraphy. He often whistled as he worked and had a deep love for music. He did bird calls, trills, warbles; his music was radiant, warm, fun. He could also play the guitar and sing. Yes, Lois was to admit after several months had gone by that she was also deeply attracted to Sol.

Sylvester noted the two often talked long into the night. In time, they announced their love for one another and a desire to be married. But for Sylvester, there was a problem. Sylvester learned through conversation that Sol and Lois were third cousins. This would never do. Cousins do not marry. Sylvester told them marriage was out of the question. It was absolutely forbidden.

They thought of eloping. But close as she was to her father, Lois told Sol she was afraid it would break her father's heart.

Sol did what he had to do. He said a painful goodbye to Lois and left the Earl home.

Not long afterward, Sol received a mission call. It was not unusual, then or now, for a male age nineteen in Mormondom and in good standing in the church to be called to serve a mission. Still, Sol wondered if Sylvester had conferred with the Brethren.

Nevertheless, Sol responded to the call without complaint. For several years he drove ox teams across the plains from Missouri to the Great Salt Lake Valley. He resisted the temptation to ever wander the gold fields of California. In its place, he was serving his faith. But he never forgot Lois. He never could.

In 1873, Sol learned that Sylvester Henry Earl had passed away. Sol wasted no time in reaching St. George. He and Lois were immediately married. (For further details of their lives together, see chapter nine.)

But there was more to the story of Sylvester Earl. He died 23 July 1873, after lying unconscious for thirty-six hours. He left this deathbed testimony, as related by son Wilber: "I have been to the world of the spirits. I have seen the Prophet Joseph and his brother Hyrum. They are very busy men. I have seen my two sons, Sylvester, Jr. and Hyrum, and they are contented and happy. I saw many others that I know. I walked the streets of their beautiful cities and saw many people. Everything seemed to be material but of a finer nature.

"I wish to leave my dying testimony with my family that they are not deceived. This is the work of the Lord that we have embraced. Joseph Smith is one of the mightiest prophets that ever graced this earth. Brigham Young is the right man to lead the people."

Then, taking Wilber by the hand, his father said, "I want you to tell my family that are not here to never disobey the counsel that comes from the authorities of this church." Sylvester then said something that surprised Wilber. "I have a message from my son Sylvester. He said to tell mother that the young lady I spoke to her about is here. I see her often and she is just as sweet and good as when in mortality. She is all the world to me and is all that I could ask her to be. I'm glad that I didn't marry the girl that I was intending, for she was not the one for me. Mother will understand when you tell her."

Lois Caroline understood. Only she and Sylvester Jr. had talked about the matter. Lois had said nothing about this to anyone for fear she might hurt the feelings of the young lady her son had dated when he was alive.

Clearly, it was a message from beyond the veil. Sylvester Henry Earl had not relinquished his great faith in the latter-day work, in death as in life.

NOTES

Jenson, Andrew. *Biographical Encyclopedia*. The Church of Jesus Christ of Latter-day Saints Library, Salt Lake City, Utah. (Also available on disk; Bookcraft, Infobase, World Classics Library, 1998.)

Earl, Sylvester Henry. Unpublished journals and autobiography in possession of the author and Earl children and grandchildren.

Wixom, Solomon Avery. Unpublished journals in possession of author and other relatives.

Shaffer, Lois. Interview at her home. Logan, Utah, January 1940.

Smith, Joseph. *History of the Church*. Salt Lake City, Utah: Deseret Book, Vol. 3., 1980.

Wixom, J. H. and Ruth S Widdison. *Wixom Family History*, Salt Lake City: Publisher's Press, 1963.

Chapter Four: Repentance
WILLIAM WINES PHELPS

"I have seen the folly of my way."

After pulling open the door of the Richmond, Missouri, jail as the food was being handed in, and then pushing the jailer down the stairs, Parley P. Pratt, King Follett, and William W. Phelps found themselves free men— at least for the moment. They soon burst into a midday crowd complete with soldiers, celebrating the Fourth of July. Shouts from the jail keeper sent the soldiers, as well as townspeople, bearing clubs, scrambling after the three Mormon prisoners now running for their lives.

The escape had been well planned, according to Parley P. Pratt's *Autobiography* (p. 251). As soon as the commotion erupted, it was a signal for friends who had been waiting in the trees not far from town to bring up horses they had hidden. The Mormon accomplices were Orson Pratt, Parley's brother, and a Mr. Clark.

In the verbose rhetoric often typical of the times, and specifically to Pratt, Parley explains it this way: "Fences were leaped or broken down in a crash; men and boys came tumbling over hedge and ditch, rushing with the fury of a whirlwind in the chase; but we kept our course for the thicket, our toes barely touching the ground . . . while we seemed to leap with the fleetness of a deer."

Each fleeing man was quickly led to a mount. But which way to go?

"'It doesn't make much difference. They've got us nearly surrounded. Each go your own way!'"

Pratt was halted briefly by a cursing Missouri gunman, but sped the other way and hid in a ravine until dark. And despite losing his horse in the excitement of dismounting to see ahead, ever alert for incensed enemies, Pratt got away cleanly to freedom in Illinois. King Follett was not quite so fortunate. Follett was taken prisoner and was returned to face the inevitable gloating and taunting. But once they determined that Follett was not a high-ranking Mormon leader, Missouri lawmen extricated him from the cursing mob and placed him in a quiet jail cell; he was released several months later. Some of his jailers even joked good-naturedly with him about his short-lived bravado.

For Phelps, there was one serious problem. His wife, Sally, had come to the prison to lend her husband moral support, but now she was also at the mercy of the mob. Phelps was not a high-profile Joseph Smith, Edward Partridge, or Sidney Rigdon—all who had been tarred and feathered by mobs at one time or another. However, Phelps had been instrumental in the rise of the Mormon faith. He had helped Joseph as a scribe in translating the Egyptian papyrus that is now found in the the Pearl of Great Price. He had assisted the prophet in almost anything requiring writing skill, particularly formal pleas to government authorities for redress. Phelps also figured prominently in taking the Mormon grievances to Governor Daniel Dunklin. History records that the latter had promised false hope that Zion's March might recover lost lands if Mormon leaders would show up and make application through the courts. As it turned out, both Smith and Phelps could have saved their time.

It was also Phelps who was printing the Book of Commandments in Jackson County on 23 July 1833, when mobs broke in and destroyed the presses. Phelps had already learned the satanic fury of Missouri violence when he was tossed out of his Independence home along with his wife, their furniture, and the printing presses. He, as did others, offered himself as a ransom—they could take his life if it would save church members who were to follow from harm. The mob turned the offer down.

Now, with Mrs. Phelps in their possession but her husband still at large, the Missouri mob cursed the woman and in Follett's presence, threatened her; but the rabble could not find it in their cruel hearts to harm an obscure female, even if she was a Mormon. Eventually, she was removed by a man who said his mother would take care of her. They "borrowed" her horse a two-week hunt for the prisoners, but after not finding any sign of them, released both her and her horse. The freed Mrs. Phelps rode to refuge beyond the Mississippi.

With danger ever lurking, Phelps hid until nightfall, but then discovered himself surrounded by mobsters eager to cause trouble. In the darkness, they hailed him thus: "Say, stranger, G-- d---, what's your name?"

Phelps wasted no time in playing their game, answering in a tone that bristled with irritation at being accosted in such a manner: "You damned rascals, what's yours!" The men sat back on their mounts to study this unexpected response. Surely, with an answer like that, he couldn't be a Mormon. Still, they weren't about to let any Mormon escape.

Phelps was not a frontier type with bent toward bawdy adventure; he was a quiet and retiring man who wrote poetry and newspaper articles. If the reader finds his language and behavior offensive, it should be remembered that the virtue selected here is repentance. Phelps had plenty to repent of, or would in short order, for upon reaching Nauvoo he was excommunicated for a variety of transgressions enumerated later.

But in order to escape, he must have acted the part of a backwoods ruffian very well. According to Parley P. Pratt, the following backwoods dialogue took place between the ruffians and their accosted traveler: "Oh, you are one of the real breed! By G-- d---, no damned Mormon could counterfeit that language; you swear real natteral; hurray for old Kentuck! But whar mou'ght you live, stranger?"

"Just up here; you mou't a kno'd me, and then again you moutn't. I think I see you a heap o' times but I've been so damned drunk at the fourth of independence, I hardly know myself or anybody else, but hurrah for old Kentuck; and what about them damned Mormons?"

"What about 'em? Egad, you'd a know'd that without axin' if you'd a seed 'em run!"

"What! They're not out of prison, are they? Out of prison!"

"Yes, the damned rascals raised a flag of liberty in open day, and burst out, and down stairs right in the midst of the public celebration, outrasslin' the damned jailer, and outrunning the whole town in a foot race. They reached the timber jist as they war overtaken, but afore we could cotch 'em they mounted their nags and the way they cleared was a caution to Crockett." One of them even said he had aimed a gun at a Mormon runaway, but "the damned cap burst" and his "powder wouldn't burn."

Responded Phelps: "Well, now stranger, that's a mighty big story and seems enemost onpossible. Did you say you cotched one a' 'em? Why I'da tho't you'd a kilt him on the spot. What have you done with him?"

"They tuk him back to prison, I suppose, but it was only the old one. If it had been one o' them other chaps we would a skinn'd 'em as quick as Crockett would a coon, and then eat 'em alive without even leaving a grease spot."

Pratt, who apparently got his information from Phelps but may have also added embellishment, tells us that Phelps stopped at a farmhouse en route to Illinois and pretended to be riding home from the big doings in town. He had gotten drunk and needed help.

Seeing his bruised face and tattered clothes, the farm owner had little reason to question Phelps's story. Phelps was provided with a straw hat to replace the one he lost and managed to reach the ferry across the Mississippi to Illinois before any of his pursuers arrived. During this lonely odyssey toward friendly faces, Phelps might well have reflected on how much he'd suffered for his belief in the restored gospel. He could have been left unmolested, even gained freedom, as would any Mormon prisoner in Missouri, by simply renouncing his religion. By so doing, he would be a local hero. Phelps might be guilty of minor peccadilloes at this time, but his testimony of the restored gospel was too firmly planted to cave in to Missouri rabble.

Nevertheless, by 17 March 1839, he found himself in big trouble with church leaders, and excommunicated. To understand how it happened, it is first necessary to know Phelps's background and how he became aligned with the Latter-day Saint cause in the first place.

Phelps was quickly converted to the restored gospel upon reading a Book of Mormon left him by Parley Pratt. Indeed, Phelps stayed up all night to compare it with the Bible. He said, "By that book [of Mormon] I learned the right way to God . . . by that book began to unfold the mysteries of God." Calling the book Pratt handed him a "glorious treasure," Phelps hastened to visit the Prophet Joseph Smith "and do the will of the Lord."

Quitting his job in 1831 as a newspaper editor in New York State, he moved to Kirtland to offer his services to the Prophet Joseph Smith. He was baptized 10 June 1831 and ordained an elder by Joseph. Phelps's name was mentioned in several early sections of the Doctrine and Covenants, promising that if he "was contrite before the Lord, he would have power to give the Holy Spirit." Yet he was told on 1 August of that same year in D&C 58:41 that, "he [W. W. Phelps] hath need to repent, for I the Lord am not well pleased with him, for he seeketh to excel and he is not sufficiently meek before me."

On 12 August, according to Joseph Smith's entry in *History of the Church* 1:203, on the third day of a canoe journey down the Missouri River, "Brother Phelps, in open vision by daylight, saw the destroyer in his most horrible power, ride upon the face of the waters; others heard the noise but saw not the vision." This is a remarkable occurrence for several reasons. Joseph records that it was Phelps (and that eleven days after being chastened in the Doctrine and Covenants) who saw the vision, not he, the prophet; nevertheless, Joseph does not question its validity.

Joseph received section 61 of the Doctrine and Covenants the next morning, warning about travel by water in this area. Interestingly, the preface explanation to section 61 says that Elder Phelps "saw the destroyer riding in power upon the face of the water," but nowhere in the 61st section is the same actually mentioned. One must turn to church history to understand what a remarkable manifestation Phelps experienced. Surely, the Lord had favored Phelps in allowing such an awful yet awesome revelation. It also indicated Phelps's propensity for receiving divine messages or warning. There would seem to be little doubt remaining for Phelps about existence of life beyond the veil.

Phelps moved to Jackson County under direction of Joseph to set up a printing press as outlined in Doctrine and Covenants 57:11–12. But after the church printing press was destroyed in Independence, Phelps grew discouraged and wrote the Prophet of the hopelessness of retaining lands, or indeed, again attempting to print sacred scripture, in Jackson County. Seeing how the Saints were being driven out and murdered, he and John Whitmer thought it practical to sell their property and move on.

David Whitmer and Oliver Cowdery tried to do so the same, an act at the time deemed to consitute a loss of faith. (Later, President Brigham Young was to sell the temple lot site in Independence for $300; but it was clear by then the property could not be retained. There was no one on hand to pay the back taxes on the temple lot site, and even if there were, the mob might at any time confiscate all such Mormon real estate in Jackson County.) Under the times and circumstances, Phelps was warned by Joseph that he was "in transgression and if he did not repent, he would be removed." The Lord had named Independence as the "land of our inheritance." Phelps felt Joseph did not understand the situation and wrote to that effect. A rift developed between himself and church leaders. For Phelps, if Zion was to be in Jackson County, or indeed, anywhere in Missouri, it would have to wait until these uneducated riffraff, fearful of anyone attempting to live a "higher" life in their presence, went away. They didn't.

At no time did Phelps rebel against the restored gospel itself. Phelps testified he had seen divine messengers in the Kirtland Temple in 1837, as indeed, many Latter-day Saints stated in all soberness during the dedication of that edifice. Phelps's hymn, "The Spirit of God," sung at the dedication of the Kirtland Temple, is indication in itself of the devotion he felt to the cause of the restored gospel with all its heavenly manifestations.

But in 1839, after his escape from the Richmond Jail, the charges caught up with William Wines Phelps. He would not follow the counsel of the prophet but fought against him. The time of his excommunication in Quincy, Illinois, was critical in church history; leaders felt it necessary to find out who was with them and who was against them. Detractors were looked at suspiciously. Confusion reigned. Several high leaders apostatized, including Thomas B. Marsh, president of the Quorum of the Twelve, Apostle Orson Hyde, and Oliver Cowdery, one of the three witnesses. Sidney Rigdon could take the heat no longer and removed himself to Pittsburgh.

With many of these once reliable men ousted, the Church sought to bring in new blood, souls who could be trusted. Ironically, such scoundrels as John C. Bennett, the elected mayor of Nauvoo, came along to fool many before their adulteries and frauds had been discovered. It was in this period of difficulty that Phelps, not faithfully aligned with church leaders, found himself out.

Phelps did not remain out of the fold long before realizing he had made a terrible mistake. Whereas he had walked in the light with hope and confidence and head held high, even when incarcerated and driven like an animal, now all was darkness before him. It was more than an intellectual void. A spirit, terrible and formidable, engulfed him. He must wholly repent of his pride and bitterness, asking humbly for readmittance to the restored gospel for which he professed love.

One of the most noble accomplishments of this man was his utterly contrite confession and desire to make amends. Suddenly separated from the glorious spirit which had buoyed him up, he sought to regain it as a man drowning desperate for air.

Orson Hyde had been in the same situation. A penitent Hyde sought readmittance to the church in 1839 and confessed his "misery in falling from the faith." He was restored and in 1841 sent on a mission to dedicate the Holy Land for return of the Jews. His period of "misery" in those two years seemed much like that felt by Phelps. He wrote the following to Joseph Smith, 29 June 1840: "I am the prodigal son although I never doubt or disbelieve the fullness of the Gospel . . . I have been greatly abused and humbled and I blessed the God of Israel when I lately read your prophetic blessing on my head as follows, 'the Lord will chasten him because he takes the honor to himself and when his soul is humbled he will forsake the evil. Then shall the light of the Lord break upon him as at noonday and in him shall be no darkness.' I have seen the folly of my way and I tremble at the gulf I have passed. So it is and why I know not. I prayed and God answered."

Phelps added that he could only hope his brethren would forgive him and allow his return to assist them in the service of the Lord. In a long letter dated 22 July 1840, Joseph welcomed Phelps back into the church, noting that his fall was the more painful because he had been a devoted servant within, not an enemy without—"truly our hearts were melted into tenderness. . . . Come on dear bother, since the war is past, for friends at first are friends at last."

So totally did Phelps endear himself to church leaders and members after his fall and reinstatement into the church that he was asked to give the eulogy at the funeral of Joseph and Hyrum after they were martyred at Carthage. It was a solemn occasion and a special privilege that only a devoted member in good standing would be asked to give.

It is not the purpose of this book to speculate on the reasons that a man such as W. W. Phelps might stray from the religion for which he had suffered so much and had obviously loved so dearly. His problems appear to begin with murmuring about church leadership in Missouri. However, only he and others like him who were there, and went through the things that he went through, including Orson Hyde, T. B. Marsh, or Oliver Cowdery, could fully answer that question.

It is obvious that a major transformation took place in Phelps's life. It was a spiritual and emotional renaissance. Phelps seemed plunged into an "abyss of despair and after groping about . . . found the scintillating light of truth." There may be no greater example of repentance and restitution out of darkness anywhere in the annals of ecclesiastical history than in the life of W. W. Phelps.

Examining the man's accomplishments, the change in his life was profound. He was, once again, trusted with important church business. William spent the entire Nauvoo period assisting Willard Richards in writing the history of the Church and as a courier conveying sensitive communications from church authorities to Governor Ford. He was with Joseph Smith the same day the prophet was shot to death in Carthage; if he had been allowed to remain in the jail, Phelps might well have been murdered with him.

On 7 October 1844, Phelps proved a strong advocate for church members to support the new leader of the faith, Brigham Young, in preparations for the exodus west. Phelps declared that Joseph had gone "but he has not left us comfortless . . . if you want to do right, support the Twelve. I will sustain the Twelve as long as I have breath."

One way to truly understand the soul of the man is to examine the songs he wrote. Fifteen are found in the modern Latter-day Saint hymnbook. Besides "The Spirit of God," there is also "Now Let Us Rejoice," "Redeemer of Israel," "Praise to the Man," "O God, the Eternal Father." The hymn "The Spirit of God" contains the memorable words known to so many Latter-day Saints: "The latter day glory begins to come forth; the visions and blessings of old are returning, and angels are coming to visit the earth . . . The Lord is extending the saints' understanding . . . the veil o'er the earth is beginning to burst." Such insightful words bearing the restoration message seem as spiritual poetry; indeed, some of Phelps's songs were originally written as poems, with music added by other church members. "The Spirit of God," however, combined both words and music by Phelps.

It would seem he equaled another composer of spiritual songs, James Montgomery, 1771–1854, who, though not a Latter-day Saint wrote "A Poor Wayfaring Man of Grief," which John Taylor sung at the request of Joseph Smith the day he was murdered in Carthage Jail, 27 June 1844. Montgomery had composed another song well received by the Latter-day Saints, "Prayer Is the Soul's Sincere Desire."

After reaching Utah, Phelps became what might be called the Leonardo de Vinci of his people. He published the Deseret Almanac in 1851, complete with astronomical observations, helped establish latitudinal and longitudinal readings for the Territory of Utah, contributed to the Deseret Horticulture Society, served many years in the State Legislature, including time as Speaker of the House of Representatives, was a member of the Utah Constitutional Convention, served on the University of Deseret Board of Regents, was a notary public, a surveyor general and engineer for Great Salt Lake Valley, a musical composer, legal counsel, a chaplain, a temple ordinance worker, and accompanied his old friend Parley P. Pratt in exploring southern Utah to determine its geography and suitability for future settlement.

He had, indeed, returned to the Latter-day Saint fold to bless it in many ways. Most importantly, by applying the principle of repentance, he had, indeed, turned around what would have otherwise been a life of darkness and despair.

Notes

Barrett, Ivan J. *Joseph Smith and the Restoration*, Provo: Brigham Young University Press, 1973.

Berrett, William. *The Restored Church*. Salt Lake City: Deseret Book, 1958.

The Church of Jesus Christ of Latter-day Saints, *Doctrine and Covenants*, Deseret Book, 1985; originally *Book of Commandments*.

Jenson, Andrew. *Biographical Encyclopedia*. The Church of Jesus Christ of Latter-day Saints Library, Salt Lake City, Utah. (Also available on disk; Bookcraft, Infobase, World Classic Library, 1998.)

Pratt, Parley Parker. Autobiography. Salt Lake City: Deseret Book, 1961.

Roberts, B. H. *Comprehensive History of Church*, Vol. 1, Salt Lake City: Deseret News Press, 1910.

Smith, Joseph. *History of Church*. Salt Lake City: Deseret Book. Vols. 1–7, 1980.

Chapter Five: Fair Play

COLONEL THOMAS L. KANE

"He was a lone voice in the East . . . "

The name of Colonel Thomas Kane flies in and out of Latter-day Saint literature. He never joined the Church, but when President Buchanan launched an army against the Mormons, it was clear that they couldn't have had a more influential friend when they needed one most.

Indeed, as a respected man in Washington's inner circles, Kane exploded many nefarious myths held up against the unpopular church. Probably thousands of people along the East Coast changed their minds about this "strange cult" because of Kane's tireless speeches and writings. Having associated with Mormon leaders and learned to both admire and respect them, he was an able and energetic spokesman for their cause at every opportunity following the Nauvoo exodus.

But why? Why go out of his way, as he once did in 1857–58, sailing all the way to Los Angeles, via the Isthmus of Panama to help a people the nation considered in rebellion and had sent the U.S. Army to attack?

Historian Donald Q. Cannon describes Kane as a well-born lawyer, diplomat, and soldier from Philadelphia who became well educated for his time and traveled in high echelon society. Kane was born in 1822. He was slightly built at 5′ 6″ and 130 pounds, but dignified looking, with deep-set eyes and a neatly trimmed beard and mustache; photos show that he appeared particularly impressive in a military uniform.

Biographers make no mention of what religion Thomas Lieper Kane might have belonged to, if any. But he became acquainted with Mormon missionaries at a Church conference in Philadelphia, 13 May 1846. He must have liked what he saw and heard because he traveled to Nauvoo to find out more about the Mormons, and within a year he terminated his military career to assist the downtrodden Saints. No other non-Mormon was as willing to follow the homeless "Camp of Israel" through the seemingly endless mud, cold, and misery of Iowa as was Colonel Kane. After meeting up with "vile border scum" in Missouri and Iowa, Kane was relieved at last to catch up with the Mormons and be in company with "persons of refined and cleanly habits and decent language."

Kane delivered an address to the Pennsylvania Historical Society in March 1850 about the Nauvoo refugees which caused considerable surprise and even scorn from a nation led to believe the Mormon people were thieves and scoundrels who didn't deserve to live in a land of decent and law-abiding Americans. After his address lauding the Latter-day Saints for their honesty and industry was published, Kane had many challengers. Hadn't all the reports from Missouri and Illinois painted followers of the Book of Mormon as a cult of counterfeiters and adulterers? Some who read the Colonel's first written address even asked for disclaimers in his second edition.

Kane did not flirt with apology. He was, in fact, annoyed. As a postscript to the second edition, he wrote, "well-meaning friends have even invited me to tone down its [the first edition] remarks in favor of the Mormons. The truth must stand alone . . . from my own personal experience, I know them [uncomplimentary rumors] to be unfounded. The purity of their character is above the average of the ordinary."

When asked by a curious audience how the Mormons became such a "refined" Christian sect as Kane said he found them, he answered they had gone through a cleansing, a purging. When driven from Illinois, "Their fair weather friends forsook them. They were willing to give up the world for their religion." Asked to explain Mormon religious doctrines, Kane demurred. "I will have nothing to do with it." Yet, later, as we shall see, he did.

Early in life, Kane seemed to be the champion of the underdog. He helped destitute fugitive slaves, underprivileged children, unwed mothers who needed a home, and "fought for right wherever he found injustice." The Mormons fit right in with the others as Kane's idea of an underdog being treated unfairly.

He told the Pennsylvania Historical Society that he knew little of Mormon industry until the day he halted his boat at some rapids along the Mississippi River. The countryside roundabout was "marred, unimproved and full of lazy, indolent, even thieving, people." But on the Illinois side he found, "half encircled by a bend in the river, a beautiful city glittering in the fresh morning sun . . . bright new dwellings, cool green gardens . . . fruitful husbandry . . . unmistakable marks of industry, enterprise and educated wealth everywhere. [It] made the scene one of singular and striking beauty." Yet, all appeared deserted. "The town lay as a dream under some deadening spell of loneliness." He visited the cemetery, finding "no signs of a plague."

Walking up the hill he discovered armed men, some sitting about in a drunken stupor, others cursing and defacing a noble marble edifice. "The high, tapering spire was radiant with white and gold." He saw it as a monument of religious worship; yet the men were engaged in "defiling," "defacing," and "desecrating" it. He was initially greeted with belligerence, for he "had been given no pass to cross the river" until assuring them he was not of the people who had been driven out. With that, they sought to curry favor and win his approval. They bragged about forcing out the builders of this resplendent city from their homes, as Kane put it, "at sword point . . . boasting greatly of their prowess." The invaders had used cannon fire to run some inhabitants from their homes and boasted of killing a father and his son. They took Kane upstairs in the temple to show him the wonderment of Mormondom's unique symbols and places where strange religious rites were performed, including a water font for "baptizing dead people." Scattered about, said Kane, were "cruises of liquor" left by the invaders.

Kane was eloquent in describing (but obviously mystified by) the Saints' love for their sacred temple—and their intense grief that they must leave it behind. Their devotion reminded him of the Jewish nation in the Roman Empire shortly after the crucifixion of Christ. He saw that the Mormons held a great reverence for the dwelling which precipitated aspirations to a higher way of life. If deluded by their zealous faith, Kane seemed to conclude that it was a "sincere delusion."

Speaking of the temple, Kane observed that "though their enemies drove them on ruthlessly, they succeeded in parrying the last sword-thrust till they had completed their gilding of the angel and trumpet on the

summit of its lofty spire." He said that anything sacred which "could pro-
voke a sneer [from enemies of the Church] had been carried off."

Returning to the river and proceeding upstream, he told the Pennsylvania Historical Society, he found some of the former inhabitants of the
ghost town in Lee County, Iowa, "those who had silenced their plows,
their hammers, their axes." Two small girls lay sobbing. Kane said rue-
fully: "Dreadful, indeed, was the suffering of these forsaken beings."
These were the last of the Mormon people to be finally thrust from the
homes they had toiled for years to build in their "Nauvoo the Beautiful."
The date: fourth week of September 1846.

However, Kane also found that wherever he went among the displaced
Saints they spoke of a hope and prayer for early spring and relief from
the winter cold. They did not feel sorry for themselves, nor waste time
lamenting their lot. Kane adds that he "was happy during this period
to move with them." He noted that "young men gave up their provided
food and shelter to the old and helpless." He saw a number of Saints who
were bruised and battered, yet worked selflessly to aid one another. He
was deeply impressed that "they laid out harvests for those who would
follow."

Many of the refugees sought work in their communities, wherever possible remaining incognito, not knowing who might be friends or enemies.
One major difference between the Old Testament Camp of Israel and that
of the Latter-day Saints was that the former had left of its own volition
and witnessed the destruction of Pharaoh's armies. The Mormons never
knew for certain in their long journey who their enemies might be.

In his address to the historical society, Kane emphasized the difference in character between the people who had been driven out of Nauvoo
and those who had driven them. He recalled that even across the river
from Nauvoo, crude shouts and cannon fire could be heard from the new
owners of the grand city that had once numbered some fifteen thousand
inhabitants.

Spiritually, however, the Nauvoo evacuees may not have been in such
lowly plight as it would seem to an outsider. John Taylor wrote in Iowa
that "we felt contented and happy—the songs of Zion resounded from
wagon to wagon—from tent to tent . . . peace, harmony and contentment
reigned in the habitation of the saints. . . . The God of Israel is with us . . .
we feel that we are doing the will of our Heavenly Father and relying upon

his word and promises." But while Colonel Kane described the victims of a cruel expulsion with praise for their honesty, clean language, courage, and industry, Governor Thomas Ford saw it differently in his *History of Illinois, 1818–1847*. He wrote following the events of 27 June 1844: "Thus fell Joe Smith, the most successful impostor in modern times, a man ignorant and coarse . . . his lusts, his love of money and power . . . dressed like a dandy, drank like a sailor, and swore like a pirate . . . he always quailed before power and was arrogant to weakness."

Of the other Mormon leaders, Ford said they were "broken down, unprincipled men of talents, to be found in every country, who, bankrupt in character and fortune, had nothing to lose by deserting the known religions and carving out a new one of their own. They were mostly infidels, who holding all religions in derision, believed they had as good a right as Christ or Mahomet . . . to create one for themselves and if they could, impose it upon mankind to live upon the labor of their dupes."

As for the rank and file, they possessed "a capacity to believe any strange and wonderful matter, if it only be new, whilst the wonder of former ages command neither faith nor reverence . . . [they were] men of feeble purpose. Some of the Mormons were abandoned rogues who had taken refuge in Nauvoo, as a convenient place for the headquarters of their villainy . . . others were good, honest, industrious people who were the sincere victims of an artful deception."

Governor Ford concluded: "Upon the whole, if one half of these reports had been true [about Mormon character] the Mormon community must have been the most intolerable collection of rogues ever assembled; or if one half of them were false, they were the most maligned and abused." It would seem difficult, indeed, to imagine that Kane and Ford were talking about the same people.

Although Ford's history was not published until 1854, years after Colonel Kane's aforementioned address, it is included here to show the widespread prejudice Kane faced in publicly saying anything good over a period of several decades about a segment of humanity that he felt was sorely misrepresented. The governor convinced many that the Mormons were a populace to be despised. But he was playing games, of course, the apparent reason being to gain favor with non-Mormon voters, who were well in the majority. Ford had conversed with Smith several times at length about problems and differences. The leader of the Mormons might be deluded in Ford's opinion, but Ford knew full well from assocations with Smith that he didn't "drink like a sailor" or "swear like a pirate."

On the other hand, Kane was running for no office, had no ax to grind, had nothing to justify, and was not seeking to win any popularity contests. For those reasons, plus the fact that he was not a Mormon, Kane appeared more credible to decision-makers in high government office. He admonished outsiders to judge the Saints according to Luke 6:43, that by their fruits ye shall know them, for "neither doth a corrupt tree bring forth good fruit."

Kane's commendatory appraisal of the Mormons was helped along in May 1844 when Josiah Quincy, former mayor of Boston (son of Josiah Sr., president of Harvard University) took an exploratory adventure west and noted several idiosyncrasies among the Saints. For one thing, no liquor was allowed in Nauvoo. For another, Joseph once pointed to four Egyptian mummies and gave the name of one, declaring that the mummy had once been a pharaoh. Quincy later wrote of such "absurdities," but he also uttered a prophecy well known in Church annals: "It is by no means improbable that some future textbook, for the use of generations yet unborn, will contain a question something like this: What historical American of the nineteenth century has exerted the most powerful influence upon the destinies of his countrymen? And it is by no means impossible that the answer . . . may thus be written: Joseph Smith, the Mormon prophet." After telling of Smith's accomplishments, Quincy adds: "such a rare human being is not to be disposed of by pelting his memory with unsavory epithets."

Quincy allowed that rogues and thieves may come and go every day, "but Smith remains a phenomenon to be explained." He added that he once heard a Methodist minister differ with Smith, who was giving a short sermon claiming that baptism was needed for man to be saved. The minister interrupted: "Wait! What about the penitent thief upon the cross who was promised by Christ he should 'be with me today in paradise?'"

"How do you know he wasn't baptized before he became a thief?" Joseph responded. Smith then kindly told the small crowd assembled to refrain from guffawing at the minister. The real answer lay in the word "paradise"; it didn't mean heaven in the original Greek but a "place of departed spirits."

Colonel Kane never attempted to enter into such intricacies of doctrine. For him, the Mormons were simply a devout and misunderstood society who were being treated unfairly and needed help with their public relations. Their plight became so imprinted upon Kane that on 13 May 1846, he wrote to Secretary of the Navy George Bancroft of intentions to abandon his military career and remain with the Mormons to champion their cause. He was present when the military called on Brigham Young to raise soldiers for the Mormon Battalion in the fight against Mexico. Kane had, in fact, earlier explained to Church leaders that President Polk wanted to help the Mormons go west at government expense. Kane carried a message from Washington to General Kearney at Fort Leavenworth that a battalion ought to be raised among the Mormons now settling at Council Bluffs. Delivery of that message appears to have been one factor in Kane heading west to be with the Mormons.

There was, of course, skepticism among the Saints. Why would a government which had previously ignored pleas for redress now try to help them? Was it to take away their men so that they would be more vulnerable to Indians and wild beasts along the way? Did they have the faith to leave their women to God's mercy? These were the Saints' initial reactions to seeing soldiers enter their camp at Winter Quarters. It is now well known, of course, that President Young approved of a "Mormon Battalion" so that money could be generated from the soldiers' pay to help the move west. Kane was a key player in facilitating President Young's plan.

Colonel Kane received many admonitions to forget the Mormons and get on with his military career." He did not heed them.

In remaining with the Mormons, did he embrace any of their beliefs? So it would seem. At Council Bluffs, after becoming ill from the wet and cold encountered in trying to catch up with Church leaders, Kane asked for and received what Wilford Woodruff calls in his Journal (pp. 25–26) a "patriarchal blessing." Since Kane remained a non-member, this is not to be confused with the blessing given members today who are first interviewed by a bishop.

The blessing was given by Patriarch John Smith in his tent. The humble circumstances didn't seem to bother the Colonel. Woodruff said he recorded the blessing as it fell from the lips of the patriarch and then handed it to Colonel Kane. Kane gave credit to the nurturing and prayers of the Saints for his surviving a close encounter with death. This visit, wrote Woodruff in his journal, "awakened feelings of gratitude toward one whose sympathies were genuine."

In the same journal, Woodruff also provides us with this insight: "President Young informed Colonel Kane that it was the intention of the Saints to settle in the Great Basin, and that as soon as they were located to apply for a territorial government. Their plans were early revealed to a tried and trusted friend." So trusted was Kane that when the telegraph arrived on the frontier, Brigham Young gave Kane his private telegraphic code number, the only person outside Church leadership to have it.

Woodruff later records a visit from O. Porter Rockwell, who was bringing mail from Nauvoo and telling of the Saints' increased suffering and abuse at the hands of mob violence. If there was ever any hope of returning to their beloved home, it now fled. The Saints turned their faces more resolutely westward. In so doing, they relied on Colonel Kane to return to Washington to speak with President Polk about the self-government they planned to set up in the Rocky Mountains. President Young even authorized Kane to recommend dimensions of the new territory that the Saints wanted to occupy.

In his manuscript history of the church, Brigham Young wrote that the Saints were greatly encouraged for a time that Kane's friendship with the president might be of help in reaching the Great Basin. "Kane's remarks [to us] have kindled up a spark in our hearts which had been well nigh extinguished."

Despite Kane's diligent efforts in the nation's capitol, however, Kane had to report a temporary failure to President Young in having Mormons governing Mormons in their new home in the west. Polk wanted his own cronies to govern Utah Territory, "many of whom," said Kane, "would oppress you in any way simply to line their own pockets. I saw it was necessary to have officers of your own people to govern you, otherwise you would be better off without any government at all."

Fortunately, after the Saints were settled and applied for territorial government in 1850, President Millard Fillmore was in office and selected Brigham Young as its first governor. Utah responded by naming a county and community after him. (Utah was also so grateful to Thomas L. Kane that it named a county after him as well, but we're getting ahead of the story.)

Kane was informed by President Fillmore that negative reports about Young were filtering back to him in Washington. Kane vouched once more for the Mormon leader's character: "I made no qualifications when

I assured you of his irreproachable moral character, because I was able to speak of this from my own intimate, personal knowledge." Many rumors had been running rampant against the Mormons since 1830 and were not easily dismissed. Some were fueled by Missouri's delegation to Congress.

But all this was just the beginning of what was to come. When James Buchanan took office and believed reports that Brigham Young was defying federal authority by refusing to recognize territorial officers, the president sent the U.S. Army to punish Utah and jail Young. Unable to convince Buchanan he was making a mistake, Kane tried by letter to convince the commander of the army, Colonel Albert Sydney Johnston, that the Mormons were law-abiding citizens. Johnston said he would not make exceptions for "rebels and traitors."

Severely ill at that time in Philadelphia, Kane got off his sick bed, against advice of family and physicians, and grew even more sick in sailing to the Isthmus of Panama, crossing overland to the Pacific and to Los Angeles. He then rode some thousand miles by horse and wagon through winter cold to confer with President Young. Page one of Kane's diary opens thus: "Homesickness and seasickness." He had left his beloved wife, Elizabeth, once again to help the Mormons. Kane apparently chose to go by sea in order to avoid Johnston and to reach Utah before the Army could arrive there. Kane traveled under the name of "Dr. A. Osborne" (the name of his black servant) to see if he would still be welcome as a stranger. He was. But being so well known by now, he likely fooled no one.

Kane also carried a message of appeal from President Buchanan asking that Church leaders take pity on Johnston's men, who were at that time trapped with dwindling rations in the deep snows of Wyoming. This was a difficult thing to lay on President Young, for with the coming onslaught of soldiers boasting what they would do to the Mormons upon arriving in Utah, President Young's men had destroyed supplies and run off hundreds of horses and pack mules. The U.S. Army was thus thwarted from coming through Echo Canyon in 1857 until the following spring.

It was an ironic request made by Buchanan and relayed by Colonel Kane: help those coming to imprison and/or kill you! Yet, President Young hearkened to the president's plea to provide at least some humanitarian effort for the troops, sending eight hundred pounds of salt, which President Young's scouts knew the general needed very much. Stubbornly, Johnston refused to accept it. This raised the ire of Texas Senator Sam Houston, who said:

"He [Johnston] sent him a taunt and a defiance . . . why could he not have said, 'I will accept it as a gift." Houston saw the act as deplorable manners on the part of a representative of the U. S. government. Houston was joined by other senators denouncing the invasion of a people already much beleaguered before reaching Utah.

In addition to accepting no help from the enemy, Johnston also had the seeming audacity (perhaps he was growing more desperate now) to send assistant quartermaster Captain Van Vliet to select a camping site in Salt Lake Valley and ask President Young if he would sell the Army beef and provisions when they arrived. President Young had had enough. He declined, making it clear that the Mormons, consistently pushed about and bullied by government leaders, would be pushed and bullied no longer. He stated, "The Mormons are supporters of the United States Constitution and love that Constitution . . . but God has set up His kingdom and it will never fall. As for any nation coming to destroy this people, God Almighty being my helper, they cannot come here." President Young promised to fight if necessary, even suggesting he would use the Indians to help, "no longer holding them by the wrist." President Young might have also wondered why the Saints' patriotism was in question, particularly since the Mormon Battalion had valiantly risen to the nation's defense only a decade earlier.

History records that Van Vliet listened intently to President Young's sincere denial that Utah was in rebellion, particularly Young's insistence that government records had been destroyed as alleged. Van Vliet told President Young that if the Army ever made war on the Saints, that he would resign, "for I will not have a hand in the shedding of the blood of American citizens." The captain promised to do his best to get an investigation into conditions in Utah. "I believe this people has been lied about the worst of any people I know." President Young told Van Vliet he believed that God had sent him to the Great Salt Lake Valley.

President Young had earlier said the same to Colonel Kane, promising Kane he would recover from his illness, for, "You cannot die until your work is done. I want to have your name live with the saints to all eternity. You have done a great work and you will do a greater work still."

Interestingly, at the time Kane was ill at Winter Quarters, he advised the Saints that if he (being a non-member) died among them, the blame would be laid to the Mormons. Fortunately, Kane recovered. One of his first acts was to intervene with the government to allow the Saints to temporarily occupy tribal lands.

Kane must have been surprised to hear President Young say, as news of Johnston's Army spread, "We are not afraid of the Army . . . the Lord would deliver us out of their hands if we do right." Was President Young possessed of a higher faith than he was? It is a matter Kane seemed to ponder deeply, stating that he "thought it very strange we [Saints] were not afraid of the Army." In the process, as a peace negotiator, Kane sometimes counseled President Young to consider accepting some government policies, so that things would go easier for the Saints. But Young's answer was always a "the Lord will provide" attitude. It must also be said there was some anxiety on President Young's part, for he called in faraway settlements such as San Bernardino to come home and help in the fight, if needed.

Kane proceeded into Wyoming to speak personally with General Johnston (recently promoted to brevet general) to relay President Young's message: "The Mormon leader only wishes peace but will not submit to any military force." Kane carried with him papers from President Young identifying him as a "peace negotiator." He also carried papers of introduction from President Buchanan, although the latter made it clear Kane acted in an unofficial, unpaid capacity. Kane was simply a mediator, no more, an unpaid volunteer seeking to intervene between his country and the Mormon Church.

When Kane arrived to speak with Johnston at Camp Scott, two miles up Blacks Fork from Fort Bridger (which by now had been purchased and burned out by the Mormons to further delay the Army), a sentry forbade Kane audience. According to an account relayed by historian B. H. Roberts, Kane was not to be denied. He had sacrificed too much to be halted by one man. Breaking his rifle butt over the sentry's head, Kane advanced to speak with Johnston.

Talk with the general went nowhere. However, incoming Governor Cummings was present at Camp Scott, and after several weeks of talk Kane convinced Cummings that there was no need to suppress a "rebellion." President Young was ready to move aside and always had been. Kane convinced Cummings he could enter Salt Lake Valley without a military escort. Smoothing the way undoubtedly was intelligence from Van Vliet that he, Buchanan, was wrong in assuming the Mormons would not seat a new governor. (By contrast, incoming Judge Eccles was not convinced. No Mormon was to be trusted.) So, minus the judge, Kane escorted the new governor into the valley. And as promised, President Young and the Saints readily accepted Cummings as the new governor.

Governor Cummings did not delay in sending the following message back to Colonel Johnston: "I have been everywhere recognized as Governor of Utah; and so far from having encountered insults or indignities, I am satisfied in being able to state to you that in passing through the settlements I have been universally greeted with such respectful attentions as are due to the representative authority of the United States in the territory."

The Mormons' apprehensions concerning Cummings dissipated after the latter wrote them, "Freedom of conscience and the use of your own peculiar mode of serving God are sacred rights . . . guaranteed by the Constitution." He would not interfere with those rights. It was a final step in erasing fears that a stranger would try to deny them ecclesiastical leadership from their esteemed prophet Brigham Young.

One final hurdle had to be cleared, however. The Saints of Great Salt Lake City had heard that their new governor was from Missouri. That did not sit well with them. Cummings quickly calmed their fears. "I am a Georgian," he said. Anywhere but Missouri was fine with his new constituents.

It was also clear by now to President Buchanan and the world that Buchanan had blundered. Probably the first historian to use the phrase "Buchanan's Blunder" was H. H. Bancroft (1875) in his *History of Utah*. Said he, "And there were many who would believe in a harsher phrase."

Clearly, Buchanan should have investigated the charges made by dissident territorial officials in Utah before dispatching a costly military force. According to Berrett, that expedition marching from Fort Leavenworth, Kansas, cost the nation's taxpayers some $20 million. A correspondent from the *New York Herald* suggested a much higher figure: "the war could escalate to some 40 or 50 million dollars." But, of course, the conflict ended more quickly and equitably than the newspaper reporter expected.

Further investigation showed the "Utah War" was fueled at least in part by anti-slavery states which didn't want Utah to enter the nation as a free state. As Bancroft put it, "People came to suspect that the invasion of "western Siberia" (Utah) was merely a "move on the president's political chessboard." In the wake of such criticism, Buchanan must have been happy for any settlement to the "Mormon problem" and grateful such a man as Colonel Kane was present to act as mediator.

Politics aside, speculation remained that Johnston's military force might yet carry out a vindictive mission against the Saints. President Young ordered his people to prepare to set a torch to their dwellings and flee should Johnston carry out any previously promised hostilities.

Said E. B. Tripp in his unpublished diary of this time, "We now make preparations to leave this place and go southwest into the desert & fire all our buildings. We are not to put in any more grain & not plant any potatoes or corn. Kane has not formed any treaty yet but . . . he [Kane] and Gov. Cummings talk of coming in."

Word of the Saints' willingness to sacrifice their beautiful city-oasis in the desert elicited great sympathy from the Eastern press, including the *New York Times* and *Atlantic Monthly* magazine. They consistently put pressure on President Buchanan to make peace with the peaceable people described by Kane. Assured by Kane that there was no rebellion, Buchanan decided to press his mistake no longer and send out a peace commission to meet with the Mormons and check out the facts. The result was that Buchanan, while listing crimes such as treason, supposedly committed by the Saints, "pardoned" the Mormon leaders. Colonel Johnston was ordered to march quickly through the valley and settle at Camp Floyd, as agreed upon with President Young, no closer than forty miles from Great Salt Lake City.

With Buchanan finally convinced there was no rebellion in Utah, he lauded Colonel Kane for his selfless, dedicated mission to negotiate peace with the Mormons. Proclaimed the president, "from motives of pure benevolence and without any monetary payment [Kane] contributed to the pacification of the territory." Buchanan, of course, seemed never to understand how simple it could have been had he listened to Colonel Kane much earlier.

Colonel Kane and his wife, Elizabeth, spent a winter in St. George as a guest of President Young. Elizabeth herself wrote many good things about Mormon life—save for a notable diffidence to polygamy. The Colonel later volunteered (the first to do so from Pennsylvania, according to one report) to fight for the Union in the Civil War. He was wounded at Gettysburg and retired from duty as General Kane.

Ironically, General Johnston, who had labeled Brigham Young a "traitor and rebel," defected from the Union to help form the Southern States

Confederacy. He was fatally wounded in 1862 fighting for the South in the Civil War.

Kane was properly eulogized by The Church of Jesus Christ of Latter-day Saints 30 June 1972, with a "heroic" size statue (nine feet tall) facing Kane's grave marker, and with a memorial chapel, in Kane, Mckean County, Pennsylvania. A similar statue is on display in the Utah Capitol Building rotunda in Salt Lake City. Elder Marion D. Hanks, a General Authority, spoke at the unveiling ceremony in Pennsylvania, as did Kane's grandson, E. Kent Kane. Said he, speaking for the Kane family, "Sometimes in the course of human events, the right man turns up at the right time."

The Church program brochure commemorating the Kane Memorial says: "For 40 years he [Kane] selflessly aided the Mormons . . . during the greatest colonization in history . . . he was a lone voice in the East against the frontier justice dealt against the Mormons." As President Young said, Kane would not die until he had performed a great work in behalf of the Latter-day Saint people. Shortly before his death in 1883, Kane wrote a letter to Salt Lake City which began, "To all my dear Mormon friends . . . " In all his charitable services rendered, it seemed he had formed no closer bond than with the exiled Saints of Nauvoo. Kane had seen fair play, championed for so many years in behalf of the Saints, triumph at last.

NOTES

Allen, James B. and Glen M. Leonard. *The Story of the Latter-day Saints*. Salt Lake City: Deseret Book, 1976.

Arrington, Leonard. "In Honorable Remembrance," *BYU Studies*. Fall 1981, 21:4, 389–402.

Bancroft, Hubert Howe. *History of Utah*. San Francisco: History Co. Publishers, 1891.

Berrett, William E. *The Restored Church*, Salt Lake City: Deseret Book, 1958.

Cannon, Donald Q. "The Historian's Corner," *BYU Studies*, Fall 1997, 18:1.

Cannon, George Q. *Life of Joseph Smith*. Salt Lake City: Deseret Book, 1964.

Kane, Thomas L. "Diary, January, 1858," Brigham Young University Lee Library, Special Collections, Provo, Utah.

Kane, Thomas L. "The Mormons: Discourse Delivered to the Pennsylvania Historical Society." King and Baird, Philadelphia, 26 March 1850.

The Church of Jesus Christ of Latter-day Saints. "Memorial tribute to Thomas L. Kane," 30 June 1972.

Nibley, Preston. *Brigham Young, the Man and His Work.* Salt Lake City: Deseret Book, 1970.

Quincy, Josiah. *Prairie State: Impressions of Illinois.* Compiled by Paul M. Angle. Chicago: University of Chicago Press, 1844. *Figures of the Past,* from the Leaves of Old Journals, Boston, 1883.

Roberts, B.H. *Comprehensive History of Church,* Salt Lake City: Deseret News Press, Vol. 3–4, 1930. (Quoting *History of Illinois,* Governor Thomas Ford, 1842–46.)

Smith, Joseph. *History of the Church.* Salt Lake City: Deseret Book, 1980.

Tripp, E. B. Unpublished diaries. Brigham Young University Lee Library Special Collection, Provo, Utah.

Tullidge, Edward. *History of Brigham Young.* New York, 1876.

U.S. Government, Congressional Records, 35th Congress, Washington.

Walker, Ronald W. "Utah's Quest for Territorial Government," *Utah Historical Quarterly,* Spring 2001, 69:2.

Woodruff, Wilford. *Journal.* Compiled by M. F. Cowley. Salt Lake City: Deseret News Press, 1909.

Young, Brigham. *Manuscript History,* several editions as cited.

Chapter Six: Resolution

BERENDINA MEIJER

"If it was a coffin, I'd know you were safe."

At the age of twenty-three, Berendina Meijer joined a strange new church without her parents' knowledge or permission. Four years later, family members learned not only of her "rebellion" but also that she planned to sail halfway around the world from both family and native land to live with strangers. It seemed an affront to both their love for her and their traditional family life in Holland.

"Dena" Meijer loved her family, but the testimony kindled within her by the Mormon missionaries burned even brighter than the day she was secretly baptized. She had prayed about it and felt strongly about her new faith. She needed to find a way to travel from Arnheim, Holland, to America. She wanted to join with other members of the Church in Zion, which was in a place called "Utah."

However, doing so would mean that she would have to quit a job most other unmarried women of twenty-seven would covet highly: traveling Europe as a "cominere," or personal attendant, to fashionable German ladies who wore clothes two or three times and then gave them away, usually to their attendants. She had all the beautiful clothes she could ever want. But she could not shake the feeling inside that she must leave it all, including her family, to reside with the "Lord's people." She began corresponding with a woman in Ogden, Utah, that the missionaries told her about—a Mrs. Weston, whose husband had served a mission in Holland. She urged Dena to come to America.

The year was 1904. Dena was told that the Mormons had built a beautiful oasis in the desert. She hoped they were right, for it would be a long voyage across the ocean. After that, trains ran from the East Coast to Ogden, Utah. If she could just be brave enough to trust what the Mormons told her.

Berendina spoke no English. She began to worry that the missionaries had brainwashed her. There were unsavory rumors circulating, and she feared that she would be met at the train by some man eager to add her to a polygamous harem, destined to become a slave wife with no hope for escape.

Were the Saints indeed led by a living prophet? Could there even be such things nowadays? What about the ruffians she would encounter in such a wild and uncivilized place as the trackless desert frontier of America?

And why would she want to throw away her cultural heritage? Holland, or more accurately, the Kingdom of the Netherlands (low countries), was a bastion, nay a legacy, of artistic refinement. Wasn't Van Gogh a Dutchman? And Rembrandt? What could she expect in the western badlands but a dearth of culture, too much dust, cowboys, and Indians? The Meijers had lived in Holland for centuries and took great pride in it. Why wasn't the Dutch Reformed Church, which had been there all that time, good enough for her?

Little similarity existed between the prevailing church of Holland and the Mormons. Reformer John Calvin, breaking away from the Lutheran Church, strongly influenced the Dutch Reformed creed, teaching that man cannot control his own destiny. They taught that a man's eternal destiny is fixed, or predestined (mankind is saved solely by Christ's grace), while the Mormons taught that good works are essential to salvation. In addition, the idea of God and Christ being two separate beings—in human form, as claimed by Joseph Smith's vision—was not only foreign to Calvinism in all its structure, but repugnant to both Protestants and Catholics since the Council of Nicea in A.D. 325. To what extent Dena's family studied Latter-day Saint teachings is not indicated in her journals. However, it would seem, at best, that they thought this American upstart religion radically different; at worst, a tool of the devil.

Dena had always thought herself the favorite of her father's six children. Yet, as he helped prepare something in which to store her things for the long journey, he told her he wished he was preparing her coffin rather than a travel trunk. "If it was a coffin, I'd know you were safe," her father told her.

There were worse things than death. Her father called Utah a place "where they have this big wall [temple grounds?] and where the Mormons are ready to clutch you." He saw Mormons as demons of some sort who looked for victims rather than Christian converts.

What was this strange Mormon urge to gather in one place, anyway? Protestants, even Catholics, were content to be faithful members where they were, prepared to bloom where planted. Why did the Mormons have to cluster to some unknown place on the other side of the world? If their daughter wanted to read her Book of Mormon, fine; she could do it here in Holland. Couldn't she?

Dena tried to explain to her family that it was the way of the Mormons, like the Jews, to gather together to share common beliefs and testimonies. They had designated a place in western Missouri as Zion, a modern-day haven for the righteous like that spoken of where Enoch lived before he was translated. But the Mormons had been run out of Missouri. So, Zion was now in Utah.

Did the missionaries know of what they spoke? Indeed, were they lying? Dena decided that the missionaries were too honest, too sincere, too look-you-in-the-eyes upright, to have misled her. The young men had bourne testimony to her—and she believed.

Elder Richard Still, of Salt Lake City, who kept a journal of his mission to Holland in 1897, shortly before Dena's baptism, paints a picture of a courteous and gracious Dutch people bound with chains of iron to their own Dutch Reformed Church. True, there were converts in the Rotterdam/ Katternburg/ Schiedam districts (near the North Sea Coast, but far from inland Arnheim) due to years of proselyting. Yet, most investigators gave one of the three following responses, according to Still's entry of 14 May 1897: (1). "This man knows the gospel is true but he was afraid if he accepted it, he would have difficulties at home"; (2) "This family seems to be interested in the Gospel but I believe they fear the ridicule of their friends"; (3) "Struck up a conversation with a man on a park bench but found he was not hungry and thirsty after righteousness."

Particularly frustrating to Elder Still was the fact that as he spoke of the Apostasy and Restoration, people peered through doorways and windows in curiosity; yet few would come listen, lest they be seen of others. Elder Still's conclusion: The Dutch people sought truth . . . but were afraid to act on it.

Elder Still also remarked, "I saw some of their so-called Christian ministers smoking their cigars and living in luxury while we, the true servants of God, must be content with our present circumstances . . . well did Jesus say, 'The foxes have holes, the birds have nests but the Son of God hath nowhere to lay his head,' but we are laying up treasures in heaven where moth and rust cannot corrupt and thieves break through to steal." The Latter-day Saint Word of Wisdom was an entirely new concept in Holland. The idea that smoking, liquor, or caffeine were banned by heavenly decree was not taught by any other religion in Europe. It would be most difficult to live.

Dena was not a minor; legally, she could choose for herself. When her ship pulled away from the dock, her mother, a small woman, fell into a dead faint. Dena received letters from relatives later saying that not long after she sailed away, her father was so frightened for his daughter that his hair "turned snow white." Dena also left behind a dear friend, Louisa, who mourned at Dena's departure.

Was she just being stubborn, as the Dutch sometimes label themselves, in insisting on going? No. She would prove the missionaries were right; then all of her family could follow her in doing the will of the Lord. She must set an example for them, and write often to share her new life in Zion. Yet, she was entering uncharted waters and she was not without apprehension. She had never been to this place called America, let alone a wilderness called Utah.

There had been earlier indications in Dena's life that she was a strong-willed woman who could face a difficult challenge on her own if she put her mind to it. When she was eleven, Dena "felt she needed more discipline" than found in her mother's home. She moved in with her maternal grandmother, Berendjie Vanderkolk, in the small village of Velp. She remained there until age eighteen, when she went to work for the aforementioned German ladies, touring Europe.

How she managed to sail across the Atlantic and find her way by train across the American continent to Utah with her language handicap is not fully explained by Dena or family journals. Since she'd borrowed money in Holland for the trip, which had to all be paid back, she didn't feel she could spend much of it. She traveled "steerage" or lower class, eating mostly food she had brought with her. Anyone observing her plight might feel it ironic. She dressed in fine clothes, which could be altered with her lap-held sewing machine, but she lived mostly on bread and water.

When she arrived in New York City, it was the Fourth of July. The Americans seemed terribly noisy and rowdy. She wondered if she'd made a mistake. Once through customs, proving she would not be an economic burden on anyone, she wondered how she could ever pay back the money she'd borrowed to her friend back home. She needed to find work in Utah immediately.

On the train trip, she did find a German girl whom she could converse with on a few subjects of mutual interest. But no one spoke real Dutch; so her talk rarely went beyond the most perfunctory of topics.

As the train pulled into the Ogden, Utah, railroad platform, Dena looked out into an array of strange faces. Then came a sudden panic. Did anyone "look" Dutch?

Meantime, Mrs. Weston also realized the dilemma at hand. "We'd better start speaking Dutch!" she exclaimed to companions. "Is dat even Hollanshe meisha?" An excited voice cried back in her native tongue: "Yes, I'm Dutch!"

Not only could she now open her soul completely for the first time on the long expedition, but at the Weston home she found more to comfort her: Dutch hot chocolate and cake. It all tasted so wonderful, she wrote. "I will never forget that day."

Dena's daughter Minnie was to later write: "When Mom came to this country (July) she came with an umbrella, her hand sewing machine, a feather mattress [apparently a fold-up], and she was very hungry."

If Dena ever felt disappointed in moving from an urban civilization to a "wild frontier," it was forgotten. Life was good in Zion. The promises made by the elders were not exaggerated. The Mormons were disciplined in spiritual matters; they were kind and loving. Her family's fears, and indeed any that she might have harbored, were totally unfounded.

Utah now reveled in statehood and its right to elect its own leaders. Polygamy was no longer an issue. Zion was growing; colonists were building up "little Zions" everywhere. Native Americans came and went as nomads, but serious threats of violence were rare. Joseph F. Smith had become president of the Church just three years before, placing major emphasis on sending missionaries to Europe. Dena had found work as a maid. She could write that the missionaries had not lied to her. All was well.

She wrote to her family, urging them to join her in Utah. After a few months her sister, Gerritje, who had joined the church earlier, made the long pilgrimage to Zion. Dena could not have been more delighted. As for her parents, though, she would have to keep trying.

Dena married Willem (later Americanized to William) Dalebout, himself a convert from Holland who had also served a mission there. The two thought they might have even seen each other at a zone conference in Holland, although they never talked to one another. Love apparently blossomed brightly, for William broke off a betrothal to another so that he might marry Dena. The Dalebouts settled first in Ogden and later in the southeast area of Salt Lake City, where they opened the Sugarhouse Bakery, and raised six children.

Dena held to the strict code of discipline and resolution that had brought her to Zion in the first place. While her husband was in Holland on a second mission, she tried to get some sewing done one day when the children began arguing over who would get a special dinner plate. There was no other adult around to help. When the noise distracted her to the point of running a needle into her finger, Dena had heard enough. She broke the plate in front of them; none would have it. Her children later said that they learned a valuable lesson.

She was sorely tried when son, Lee, age seven, didn't come home on time to do his chores. Among other things, he had wood to cut. Instead, he went with an older boy into town and was prevailed upon by his companion to shoplift a pencil. When he came home late, he was afraid to take his cap off, for his mother had taught him, "When you tell lies, they are written on your forehead." He pulled his cap down over his forehead, for he knew he was about to tell a lie.

Lee then tried to hurry up to bed. But mother wanted to talk, or rather for her son to talk. Soon he had to tell her everything. He was in tears. After "getting his expected talking to," Lee chopped the waiting wood and went to bed, thinking it had "blown over." But next day, Dena walked her son to the store (there was no money for a street car) where he had stolen the pencil. Said Mrs. Dalebout in her thick Dutch accent: "I vaunt to see store manager."

The manager listened politely, "Well, boys will be boys," he said.

This would never do. Mrs. Dalebout thrust hands to hips, insisting that Lee "learn his lesson." The boy spent the next two weeks working at the store for two hours a day. Afterward, Lee wrote in a family journal, "I have never stolen anything since." Later, Lee would become a chaplain and counselor for people who had engulfed their lives in crime and tangled emotions.

A daughter-in-law, Gladys Dalebout, describes Dena as adhering in every way to the religion for which she had sacrificed so much; yet for a time, self-conscious of her poor English, she would not attend church. Only after feeling more proficient with the new language did she socialize with other members.

A granddaughter, Judene (whom Dena always called "Yudene"), recalls her as a buxom woman, with blonde hair worn in a bun, stern yet kindly. She gave out nickels from a kitchen drawer to grandchildren, but not without reason. The nickel was always a reward for something well done.

Mrs. Dalebout was also highly skilled in tatting beautiful hankies and in crocheting. "Yudene" said Dena gave her a lesson one day in crocheting. "I'd learned how to knit at Primary, so I was confident I could pick it up easily. I watched her fingers fly in tiny circles as she did a chain, then a shell. She asked if I was ready to try. Of course, I was. I eagerly took the thread and hook in hand . . . in the same manner for knitting."

"Oh, Yudene!" her grandmother exclaimed. "Not like der 'futeball' player!"

"I'm sure grandmother forgave me but after she said what she did, I was disappointed in myself," said Judene years later.

Dena's son, Alma, "Yudene's" father, somehow contracted rheumatic fever as a young boy. Dena's later journals are filled with accounts of trying to nurse the boy to health by carrying him from window to window to receive maximum sunlight. It is not known if this had any positive medical impact on the young lad but the spirit behind it was recounted later: "I was one thankful boy . . . for the loving care she gave me." Alma also beheld his mother's penchant for honesty. When a wallet was found, an ad was placed in the paper to find the rightful owner.

Another son, Bill, recalled her mode of punishment: not spanking, staring. Staring hard. "When she looked at me like that, it was worse punishment than if I had been given a whipping."

On Christmas Day, the extended family had a tradition of gathering at Dena's small home around 11 A.M. Everyone exchanged gifts; but the traditional highlight was when she served Dutch-style hot chocolate and raisin bread. Writes Judene, "The last Christmas we gathered in such a way was just before she passed away. She had been ailing for a long time. Her husband was by now gone and with her faith, she was ready 'to go on her trip' to see 'Pa' again."

"That Christmas she gave personal treasures to each of us," said Judene. "I got her wrist watch. It hasn't worked for years. But I'd never give it up."

Yes, two years after Dena came to America, all of her family, including her "Ma" and "Pa," had joined The Church of Jesus Christ of Latter-day Saints and gathered with her in Zion.

A resolute Dena had led the way. Now, all were together again and exactly where Dena knew that the Lord wanted them to be.

NOTES

Meijer, Berendina. Unpublished diaries, in possession of Mrs. Gladys Dalebout, Salt Lake City, Utah, unless otherwise quoted.

Dalebout, Gladys and family. Personal interviews, Salt Lake City, 9 February 2000.

Still, Richard. Unpublished diary, mission to Holland, 1897–1900, Provo, Utah: Brigham Young University Lee Library, Special Collections.

Chapter Seven: Trustworthiness

DANIEL WELLS *and* LOT SMITH

They had made a promise to Brigham Young;
and they would keep it, even if cost them their lives.

They'd defeated Mexico not long before and in fact, had never lost a war. Now, Colonel Albert Sydney Johnston and 2,500 of the world's best trained soldiers marched toward Utah and the rebellious Mormons.

The Mormons had the dynamic duo of General Daniel Wells and Major Lot Smith, plus a few officers, and a fluctuating supply of volunteer manpower. The Mormons also had a handicap. Johnston's troops were trained to shoot to kill. Wells and Smith had express instructions from President Brigham Young to harm no one. It was a mammoth responsibility with which they had been entrusted. Yet Wells and Smith prevailed in what was probably the most unusual military "battle" ever waged.

The year: 1857. Convinced Mormon leaders had refused to recognize territorial appointees, President James Buchanan was determined to quell the Mormon "rebellion" and depose Brigham Young as governor. As for Brigham, he was convinced that if the army could be kept from entering the valley until spring (with no one killed thus far), chances were good a serious misunderstanding could be corrected and peace negotiations effected. Obviously, much depended upon the personal savvy and trustworthiness of Daniel Hanmer Wells and Lot Smith to carry out Brigham's orders, despite being in such grave danger themselves.

As a non-member in Nauvoo, Wells had witnessed the war between Mormons and their enemies up close and personal. He'd been deeply moved by Joseph Smith's compassion for the Saints and how those who died without hearing the gospel might be saved. Wells was convinced Joseph Smith was a great spiritual leader inspired from on high. He developed a deep love for the teachings of Smith and came to believe fervently in the Mormon cause, joining The Church of Jesus Christ of Latter-day Saints 9 August 1846. It was a time of great peril, for the last Mormon refugees were being driven across the Mississippi at gun and cannon point.

Mobs descending upon the city would have surely bypassed Wells had he not announced himself a Mormon. But in joining the Saints, Daniel would suffer with them. Much of material value was sacrificed; he had owned much acreage in the Commerce area, including part of the temple lot site, all of which were offered to the Saints at a fair price when they fled Missouri. Later, President Young couldn't help but notice that Wells was both devoted and skillful in helping the Saints make their mass exodus from Nauvoo in safety.

Wells's greatest service was in bolstering the morale of a weary people besieged with the overwhelming forces of an enemy bent on their destruction. According to historian B. H. Roberts, Wells was such "a tower of strength" in holding back hostile mobs that he earned the title "Defender of Nauvoo." Wells was among the very last to leave the besieged city, helping poor and ailing evacuees all the way into Iowa.

In the mass exodus, Daniel must have possessed a firm testimony of the restored gospel, for it cost him his wife and son. His wife (no name is given) refused to go with him; nor would she allow her son to go. Daniel never saw either one of them again.

Wells was described by his son Junius as a tall, distinguished looking man with extremely deep-set eyes, a rather long nose, a prominent forehead, and jutting chin; he had a "commanding stature" that invited attention. Wells had learned at an early age how to deal with challenge. His father died when he was twelve, leaving him to care for a mother and younger sister. As the MIA Manual of 1906–07 put it, Wells "did a man's work for a boy's pay." According to biographer Hinckley, Daniel learned from his boyhood how to deal with ruffians and trouble-makers.

It was logical then that Wells, by now risen to the rank of Lieutenant General in Utah's reorganized Nauvoo Legion, would be tapped by President Young to lead the military effort against Johnston's Army. Daniel got his "battle plan" going 1 August 1857, a week after learning of Johnston's advance from Fort Leavenworth, Kansas. Wells set about impressing upon his men President Young's resolute directive: Johnston must not set foot in Salt Lake Valley. But this must all be accomplished without bloodshed.

Major Lot Smith was a mere twenty-seven years old when he accepted command of forty-four men from General Wells to enter the "Utah War." At age sixteen, Lot was the youngest member of the Mormon Battalion. His mother, Rhoda Hough Smith, told her son that he was too young to join the march against Mexico; the minimum age listed by the U. S. Army was eighteen. Yet we learn from Smith family journals and records that Lot appealed to his mother to pray about it. She did. And the answer she got was that her son should not be denied the opportunity to fight for his country and help the cause of the Latter-day Saints desperately trying to reach the West. When the boy presented himself to President Young and military leaders, the first reaction was to turn him down. But they decided he was large of stature, emotionally mature for his age, and that exhibited the positive attitude needed. An exception was made for the young lad named Lot Smith.

Lot was born in Oswego County, New York, in 1830, the same year the Church was organized. In Nauvoo, 7 April 1844, while with a sister at age fourteen, he was impressed by Joseph Smith's famous King Follett discourse on the plan of salvation. The other members of his family were already church members. Lot joined them.

One photograph shows Lot in full beard, with a rugged, tanned look, high forehead, determined chin, and penetrating, almost burning eyes. He had a look that seemed to say he would not be denied what he set out to do. And according to Latter-day Saint historian William Berrett, Lot followed through. He was "remarkably successful in all he was asked to do."

Lot's long march in the Mormon Battalion to the West Coast was filled with grueling days of sand and sun, an attack of wild bulls, with the engagement of Mexico's hostiles a constant threat. But he was also promised by Brigham Young that none would be harmed. "They would have no fighting to do." This came to pass as prophesied. However, one tragedy did occur for the young Smith boy. He learned when the battalion reached San Diego that his mother had died. This must have been especially hard for him; she had been a special inspiration in his life. Now, he was on his own.

The young man's grit and fearless demeanor, combined with a deep spirituality, impressed peers throughout the Battalion's long march. He was never heard to curse or use foul language; and he seemed always to find a way to get any task assigned him completed without excuse or complaint. Perfect for Brigham Young's army. (There seems a touch of irony here in Lot fighting for and then against the same U. S. Army.)

Smith was asked by General Wells if he was up to the task of burning Army supply wagons without harm to the soldiers or himself. Nothing would be provided for him. He would have to "board at the expense of Uncle Sam." It is typical of his character that Lot answered, "Yes, he thought he could do that."

One of Major Smith's assignments was to utilize the tactical skills of Orrin Porter Rockwell. Rockwell carried no military rank. He reportedly sometimes drank to excess, used profanity, and cussed at his superior officer. But Major Smith never complained publicly of it, apparently happy to have someone with Rockwell's courage and devotion to a righteous cause matching his own. Said Lot, "Rockwell and I were good friends on the following basis: I did as I pleased and he regularly damned me for it."

But Rockwell can't be blamed for being cautious. After all, he had languished for months in Missouri and Illinois jails. He was not about to "walk into another trap."

On one occasion, peering down upon several hundred head of cattle grazing serenely below, Major Smith gave the order to attack and disperse the animals. Rockwell let out a stream of curse words against Smith. It had to be a setup. Soldiers were, sure enough, waiting in the willows and bushes but not in sufficient number to stop Smith. The latter rode in boldly, scattered the guards, hidden or otherwise, and sent what cattle he could back to Utah. (Nothing here is meant to belittle the many accomplishments of O. Porter Rockwell. His activities in the Utah War are well covered, however, in other biographies, including one by Van Alfen, referenced at the end of the chapter.)

Other officers such as Colonel Robert T. Burton played a strategic role in going out in August of 1857, ostensibly to protect Latter-day Saint immigrants; but his real purpose was determining strength and location of the enemy. He reported the same to Smith and Wells on a regular basis.

General Wells placed fortifications in Echo and East canyons, along the route followed by the original pioneers across Big and Emigration canyons into the Great Basin. From these fortresses (which can still be seen today) the defenders could roll down boulders to halt the enemy's advance.

The war placed a double burden on Wells. Following the death of Jedediah M. Grant, Wells was named on 24 January 1857 as President Young's second counselor. In this he must serve both as a sensitive confidante and spokesman, as well as top military combatant.

Based on information from officers Wells and Smith, President Young wrote on 30 September 1857, "It is a solemn time. The armies of the Gentiles are making war upon us, and we have to defend ourselves against a nation of 25 millions of people, and the war has just commenced. We have to trust in God for the result. We shall do what we can, and leave the work in His hands."

In his correspondence to the troops, Wells cited the "blessings of the Almighty," and showed his vast wisdom by stating, "the good never wish for war, and the wise are always ready for it." President Brigham Young couldn't have said it better himself.

As the Army moved into Wyoming, Young determined that Johnston must not be allowed to benefit from church-owned Fort Bridger and Fort Supply, twelve miles to the east on Smith's Fork. The first was bought from Jim Bridger and the latter was built as a rest stop for incoming Mormon immigrants. Both forts were burned out on 2 October, as ordered by President Young. In minutes, four years' work went up in smoke. All adjacent grasslands were also torched. The value of the two forts, according to historian Preston Nibley was Fort Bridger, $2,000 and Fort Supply, $50,000; but it was $300,000 total, if relying on historians Fred Gowans and Eugene Campbell who calculated going wages at the time for the multiple improvements.

Upon seeing Fort Bridger in ashes, veteran frontiersman Jim Bridger, acting as guide for the Army, was said to swear mightily against President Young and call him a robber. Jim had a short memory, for the Mormons had paid Bridger $8,000 for it two years earlier. Even then, the mountain man was to later seek $600 a year from the Army for leasing rights.

Meticulous instructions from General Wells to all Utah militia officers, dated 4 October 1857, addressed the challenge: "You will proceed with all possible dispatch, without injuring your animals, to the Oregon road, near the bend of Bear River north by east of this place. Take close and correct observations of the country on your route . . . send scouts ahead to ascertain if the invading troops have passed that way. [If so] take a concealed route and get ahead of them . . . annoy them in every way possible. Use every exertion to stampede their animals and set fire to their trains. Burn the whole country before them and on their flanks.

"Keep them from sleeping by night surprises; blockade the road by felling trees or destroying the river fords where you can . . . keep your men concealed as much as possible and guard against surprise. Keep scouts out at all times and communications open with Colonel Burton, Major McAllister, and O. P. Rockwell who are operating in the same way. Keep me advised daily of your movements, and every step the troops take and in what direction. God bless you and give you success. Your brother in Christ, Daniel H. Wells. P. S. . . . Take no life, but destroy their trains and stampede or drive away their animals at every opportunity."

There have probably never been such benign instructions as these in the annals of military conflict. There may never be again.

Under orders from Wells, as explained in Smith's narrative, found in *Contributor Magazine*, Lot and his men rode all one night in early October to reach a supply train commanded by a wagon master named Dawson. Smith made no attempt to be clandestine. He rode right up. "Mr. Dawson, my men are here to burn the wagons of your train."

Dawson was astonished. "For God's sake, don't burn the trains!"

"It is for His sake that I am going to burn them," Lot replied boldly.

While talking with the wagon master, a messenger came in from Colonel Johnston. Smith stopped him in his tracks. Warning the courier not to skip a word, Smith ordered him to read it. The message: "There are Mormons about . . . be sure to remain awake and alert."

Lot allowed, sure enough, that it was an appropriate warning. He and his men had at times in fact, found the soldiers loud, profane and also drunk. Lot told Dawson and his men to gather their personal belongings from the wagon. Then he initiated a giant bonfire which must have made quite a spectacle on the prairie horizon.

The next day, 4–5 October 1857, Maj. Smith encountered wagon master Simpson. "I told him that I came on business. When I demanded his pistols, he replied 'By G-d, sir, no man ever took them yet, and if you think you can, without killing me, try it.'" Smith did. Without a shot fired. He commandeered the man's weaponry by assuring the wagonmaster he had no chance. His teamsters had already surrendered their firearms. Lot wasted little time arguing with Simpson. "It would only take a minute [to kill you] but I do not like blood." Simpson lamented that he hadn't killed the freighters himself for giving up so easily. Said Lot: "He was terribly exercised over the capture of his train . . . with its cowardly teamsters."

The men were not soldiers but concessionaires hired by contract; they had little quarrel in fighting anyone. Smith must have suspected as much, and felt that if he was firm enough with them, they'd back off, which they did.

Simpson pleaded with Lot to wait until he was out of sight before burning the wagons so that the report he must make to Colonel Johnston would be easier. Smith wrote in his journal the following:

"To view the carnage and do nothing about it might ruin his reputation as a wagonmaster. Smith: "I told him not to be squeamish, that the trains burned very nicely. I had seen them before and that we hadn't time to be ceremonious. We then supplied ourselves with provisions [from the government], set the wagons afire, and rode on about two miles from the stream [Big Sandy] to rest."

One reason the trains "burned nicely," as Smith put it, was that they carried sulfur and saltpeter (potassium nitrate), both chemicals any child might ignite rather easily. Smith also directed a friend, Jack Bennington (a non-Mormon who had worked at Fort Leavenworth and helped spread the word that an army was heading to Utah), to set the wagons ablaze. Said church member Smith: "It was appropriate that a gentile torch the wagons of the gentiles."

Later, Lot directed one Bill Hickman to drive some thousand head of U.S. cattle to Salt Lake Valley. Some of the civilian teamsters defected to go along with him. With this destruction, Johnston's men, (according to Mormon spies in their midst) renewed threats to pillage and ravage the valley of the Saints upon arrival. Most assuredly, they would send Brigham Young, and all with more than one wife, to the gallows. Latter-day Saint John Taylor was to tell Vice President Schuyler Colfax in 1869, "We had men in all their camps to see what was intended. There was a continual boast among the men . . . farms, property, women were to be distributed. Beauty and booty were their watchword. We were to have another grand Mormon conquest."

Some of these spies posed as emigrants heading for California. Others were teamsters (civilians providing supplies) who lost heart for the unsavory business of war, going on to Salt Lake Valley. Some soldiers, out of sympathy, told Lot's couriers all they knew. If caught, of course, such a "traitor" could have been hanged on the spot for treason.

Smith kept busy. In one account he kept, he burned 74 supply wagons, and ran off some 1,000 head of cattle, without harming a single man, woman, or child. Lost to U.S. troops, according to their own reports, were 68,820 rations of dry vegetables, four tons of bread, four tons of coffee, eighty-four tons of flour, forty-six tons of bacon, 3,000 gallons of vinegar (which was apparently used to season food and/or in pickling and processing fruit) and seven tons of soap. How the men remained in good health, with so many supplies destroyed must have been a matter of vexation. Mules and horses needed to carry supplies were also run off.

So successful was Smith, keeping to a regimen of daily prayer and surreptitious warfare, that a soldier later confided he thought the major commanded at least 500 men. To further this false notion, Lot placed men on skylines, built fires at night, and vanished to reappear as a new force.

Johnston wrote to Army headquarters 30 November 1857 that his troops were in good spirits, "although some are experiencing frostbite." He blames inclement weather for slow progress, not the Mormons. The soldiers are "young, active and hardy men, generally good shots." Johnston seemed hardy enough. But he, or other officers in charge at the time, appear to have been poor tacticians in allowing unguarded supply trains to proceed apart from the soldiers. Either that, or someone underestimated the Mormons' will to resist.

After Lot's lightning hit-and-run raids with a few good men, it soon became clear to Johnston that he was up against dedicated men with devastating guerrilla tactics. The U.S. Army, which had departed via Colonel Edmund Alexander's vanguard troops at Fort Leavenworth 17 July 1857 (and which were now commanded by Johnston) were by December hopelessly bogged down with no hope of getting through the deep snow of Echo Canyon until spring. At one point, it was decided to attack from the north up Hams Fork to Fort Hall, Idaho, on the Oregon Trail, then south to Utah. But deep snow changed that plan. Johnston ordered all his troops in to bivouac near Fort Bridger.

Salt Lake Valley was ideally situated to prevent wagons from attacking down the narrow confines of Echo Canyon. No amount of snow however, seemed to deter Smith and the other defenders from moving back and forth at will on horseback. Of course, they knew the terrain, knowing which mountain ridges were swept by wind or snow, and of course, were more mobile than the baggage-laden army.

As the winter of 1857–58 bombarded southwestern Wyoming, Johnston focused on sheer survival. Not only was snow growing deep along the Green River/Hams Fork/Blacks Fork country (reaching up to 7,000 foot elevation), but temperatures had dipped as low as 44 degrees below zero. It was enough to make the soldiers ponder the necessity of their mission. And to make them more angry at those who had sent them, as well as those who now hindered them.

No doubt the phantom raids of Major Smith played a disheartening role in the soldiers' minds. Lot was nearly captured only once and he wrote in his journal (*Lot Smith's Story*, pp. 15–20) that it made him "mad," for it seemed a subterfuge. He had ridden boldly up to Captain R. B. Marcy, whereupon Marcy asked Lot, "What is your business out here?" To which Lot replied, "Watching you." To which Marcy explained he was searching a way to Utah. Smith: "Nonsense. You have left the main road to the valley long ago."

Marcy only smiled and said the administration "did not want to come to blows with the people of Utah." In no mood to be trifled with, Smith rebuked that statement by saying the Army had put the Mormons in the position of holding off a man with knife meant to cut [our] throat."

As Lot's men rode away, Marcy suddenly sent his soldiers after them. Smith saw that a steep stream bank loomed ahead. His men were surrounded on three sides. But at the last second, Lot found a ravine cut into the bank. An undaunted Smith wrote in his journal, "We rode away leisurely up the hill."

A short time later, Lot was attacked again by soldiers, who killed a horse they thought was Smith's mount. Thinking they had him at their mercy, the soldiers sent up a shout. But it proved not to be Smith's horse. Lot's men, in making their escape, fired the only Mormon shots of the war. But no one was hurt on either side.

Clearly, Lot's destruction of wagon supplies was being sorely felt by the Army, even by early winter. Johnston was so desperate he sent Marcy on 24 November all the way to New Mexico to gather clothing and supplies. Marcy had been cautioned to go slow and watch for Mormon guerrillas. He did not get back until mid-June as Johnston was marching into Salt Lake Valley. Thus, Marcy's supplies were not available to Camp Scott.

Marcy's adventure indicated just how much Smith's raids had crippled the government's military campaign.

Johnston had been forced to build Camp Scott, two miles up Black's Fork from Fort Bridger, when the fort was discovered in ashes. Throughout the lonely winter, Mormon Captain John R. Winder with a small band of Mormon men daily climbed a ridge in Echo Canyon to check for clues of any advancement toward the west. When none was seen, President Young sent the weary men home to spend the winter with their families. Except for a few who maintained a constant vigilance, ready always to harass any advancement of troop, the Mormon defense temporarily rested.

On one occasion, Smith showed total disgust for a cowardly attitude among his men. He heard that two Mormons were being chased by two soldiers. "Then I hope they catch them. I don't want any men [working for me] who can be chased by two other men." Another time when it was rumored soldiers were nearby, and some thought it prudent to run, Smith said he would kill the first man who moved. Given Lot's known concern about avoiding bloodshed, it was most likely a bluff. But Smith's tough stance paid off. The men held their ground and were not harmed.

The only Mormon wounded in the war (no soldiers were harmed, at least not by Latter-day Saint hands) picked up a U.S. Army musket that through some defect, exploded in his hands. Smith personally did what he could for the man, getting him back to Salt Lake City for medical treatment.

The Mormons' daring deeds, as described in Washington legislative circles, seemed to be supported in the Eastern press. It seemed even Mormons were allowed to defend themselves. But to Johnston and Buchanan, the wagon burning was one more proof of treason.

Much has been said of Bill Hickman committing murder under orders of Brigham Young during (and even after) the Utah War. Both novelist Vardis Fisher and a Hollywood film on the life of Brigham Young claim Hickman did "hit" (murder) assignments for the Mormon leader. This is refuted by historians Leonard Arrington and Hope A. Hilton in *Bill Hickman: Setting the Record Straight*. They say that Hickman, at least during the Mormon War, simply did his duty.

According to Wilford Woodruff's journal, p. 404, Smith's enemies spoke well of him. "The wagonmaster (not named) of that [burned] train said Lot Smith and his men were gentlemen. And it was one of the wisest and best things that Gov. Young could have done, for it stopped the progress of the Army until events so changed that peace came. It prevented the shedding of blood on either side and sent him [the wagonmaster] back to the States where he could escape the suffering of the soldiers who wintered in the mountains."

Due to the careful planning of Smith and his cohorts, no federal guards or scouts ever harmed the guerrilla warriors, and no sabotage efforts were suddenly discovered in a way which forced the taking of life, even in self-defense.

Wilford Woodruff wrote in his journal that the men were protected by Divine Providence: "The soldiers shot many balls at our men from time to time and those balls fell like hail around the servants of God but not a drop of their blood has been shed, neither did the brethren return fire upon the enemy. . . . Fear had so taken hold of the soldiers that they would flee into the main body of the Army at the approach of a small number of our brethren."

Again, according to Woodruff's journal, "A Brother Maxwell, who had been in charge of a small scouting party . . . felt strongly impressed that danger confronted him and his camp." Against his men's protest, he moved camp; soon afterward, several hundred men surrounded the place but found it empty." On another occasion, Colonel Allen of the Mormons was captured and threatened by Johnston with hanging. Allen took off his boots, pretending to warm his feet by the fire. When the soldiers let their guard down, Allen leapt from the firelight and got away in his stocking feet.

When incoming Governor Alfred Cummings was persuaded by Colonel Thomas Kane to enter Great Salt Lake Valley and peacefully take over his rightful appointment, and with Johnston's Army in its rightful place 40 miles away, it was clear Daniel H. Wells and Lot Smith, with other defenders, had completed a most worthy work of preserving the peace.

Historian H. H. Bancroft tells us that peace came just in time, for in the spring of 1858 Buchanan was considering mustering a total force of 8,000 soldiers to put an end once and for all to the Mormon "rebellion." But everywhere people were asking this question: why were the Mormons so willing to fight so devotedly, if they had not a just cause? If the president couldn't see it, the media could, and so could most Americans following the Utah saga.

As history attests, President Buchanan pardoned Mormon leaders, chastening them, it is true, but pardoning them nonetheless. In the process, the president gave Wells, Smith, and other defenders unintended compliments to wit: "While the troops were on their march, a train of baggage wagons, which happened to be unprotected, was attacked and destroyed by a portion of the Mormon forces, and the provisions and stores with which the train were laden were wantonly burned. In short, their present attitude is one of decided and unreserved enmity to the United States and to all their loyal citizens . . . overt acts of the most unequivocal character."

The president reminded the Mormons that the lands obtained from Mexico, including Utah Territory, were purchased by their U.S. Government (at a cost of $15 million). "This is rebellion against the government to which you owe allegiance." The president's almost comedic indictment/pardon indicates all the more how uninformed the president was about the Mormons' loyalty. (Hadn't the Mormon Battalion entered the war most patriotically against Mexico, the U.S. enemy?) In ordering Johnston and his Army to pass peacefully through Salt Lake Valley, not a single soldier stepping out of line, Buchanan, given sufficient time, finally seemed to recognize the truth.

Things worked out precisely as President Young envisioned. Johnston was delayed and President Buchanan had time to listen to reason. Although oft vilified by historians, and even voted in a January 2000 *Readers Digest* poll as the nation's "worst president," Buchanan was, according to the *World Book Encyclopedia*, an active Presbyterian who refused to use force in holding seven of the fifteen slave states in the Union. With them, he showed restraint, seeking negotiation rather than war. Increasingly, however, he had to deal with the slavery issue and may have in actuality, paid too little personal attention to the "Mormon problem." Perhaps he should have.

Lot later served a mission to England and two terms in the Utah Legislature. He went on to become the first sheriff of Davis County. Under an appointment from President Lincoln to Brigham Young, Lot also guarded mail routes and telegraph wires between Utah and Missouri. Under President Young's orders, he helped colonize the Little Colorado River country of eastern Arizona where he served as a stake president. When Wilford Woodruff visited in 1890, the gritty Lot guided Woodruff through several blizzards to witness religious rites of Navajo and Moqui (Hopi) tribesmen. Woodruff was to write that Lot was both a worthy guide and a brother.

Later, Lot moved to Tuba City, Arizona. By this time, he had seven wives and was on the dodge from federal marshals seeking "polygs." But danger lurked from another source. On 21 June 1892, while trying to protect livestock, Lot was shot in the back by a renegade Navajo; he died later at home. "Renegade" was the term used by older Navajos lamenting the act which "had taken from them a good friend." The shooting was something of an aberration for the time, since in 1874, Jacob Hamblin had met with the Navajos in their homeland with a peace treaty signed and honored thereafter throughout southern Utah.

Lot was buried near Tuba City, then ten years later reinterred in the Farmington, Utah, cemetery where a eulogy was delivered by Joseph F. Smith. The deceased was remembered as a "generous, noble-hearted man. In every instance, he discharged his duty to the best of his ability." Another eulogy from John Winder, who knew Lot's role in the Utah War: "His men loved him; he was always in the lead." The Mormon community had lost a dedicated man who could be entrusted with a difficult task and let nothing stand in his way of accomplishing it.

Lot's descendents gathered in Farmington, Utah, to commemorate the well-founded trust Brigham Young placed in him and add to his legacy at his cemetery marker. He was also honored 23 June 2000, for his role in rounding up and branding wild horses for the Church on Antelope Island. As the *Deseret News* of 20 June 2000 put it, "Lot Smith is about to receive some long-due recognition." If he had been something of a forgotten man for his many years of service and accomplishment, such was no longer the case.

When General Wells was called to be President Young's second counselor, he was tabbed by Latter-day Saint historian Preston Nibley as a man of "strength, dignity, with a wealth of experience, a thorough knowledge of the Gospel, and a loyalty to the Church and to President Young that was unquestioned. He was a gentleman, scholar, executive, a military man, mild in manner, yet absolutely fearless."

He served a mission to England, was president of the European Mission, mayor of Salt Lake City in 1866–76, and chancellor of the University of Deseret. He dedicated the St. George Temple, and was President of the Manti Temple. The community of Wellsville, Cache County, was even named after him. On 2 September 1877, Wells was the first speaker at the funeral of his old friend, Brigham Young, the "Lion of the Lord."

When Wells died 29 March 1891, he was honored by many church dignitaries: President Woodruff delivered a eulogy; the Twelve Apostles were honorary pallbearers; Joseph F. Smith gave the grave side dedicatory prayer. Daniel's wife, Emmeline, a remarkable woman of public service in her own right, who campaigned tirelessly on the East Coast for womens' rights (and whose statue stands in the Utah Capitol Building rotunda), read a poem to her husband's memory.

Wrote the family in a memorial tribute: "His voice was not good for public speaking, nor his manner eloquent but his discourse was fervently religious and loyally patriotic, abounding in truth and common sense. . . . [He was] pure in heart, merciful, generous, affectionate, patient, courageous, faithful and true."

Like his colleague Lot Smith, Daniel Wells was worthy of the highest trust. General Daniel H. Wells stated that it was interwoven into his character "never to betray a friend, a brother, my country, my religion or my God."

NOTES

Allen, James B. and Glen M. Leonard. *The Story of the Latter-day Saints*. Salt Lake City: Deseret Book, 1976.

Arrington, Leonard and Hope Hilton. "William 'References Bill' Hickman: Setting the Record Straight," *Task Papers in LDS History*. No. 28, 1979.

Bancroft, Hubert Hugh. *History of Utah*. San Francisco: History Co. Publishers, 1891.

Barrett, Ivan J. *Major Lot Smith, Mormon Raider*. American Fork: Covenant Communications, 1991.

Berrett, William E. *The Restored Church*. Salt Lake City: Deseret Book, 1949.

Craig, Mrs. Deanne. Diaries and journals in possession of her late husband, Elias, a grandson of Lot Smith, as well as two interviews at her home. Provo, Utah, 5 November 1989; 8 January 1990.

Godfrey, Kenneth, et al. *Women's Voices*, Salt Lake City: Deseret Book, 1982

Gowans, Fred and Eugene Campbell. *Ft. Bridger.* Provo: Brigham Young University Press, 1936.

Hinckley, Bryant S. *Daniel H. Wells.* Salt Lake City: Deseret News Press, 1942.

Jenson, Andrew. *LDS Biographical Encyclopedia.* Salt Lake City: The Church of Jesus Christ of Latter-day Saints, 1901, pp. 803–806.

The Church of Jesus Christ of Latter-day Saints publications: MIA Manuel, "Lot Smith," 1906–07, SLC, Utah. *Contributor Magazine*, several volumes as indicated.

Marcy, R. B. *Thirty Years of Army Life on the Border.* New York: Harper and Bros., 1866.

Newspapers: *Deseret News, New York Times*; Periodicals: *Atlantic Monthly*

Nibley, Preston. *Brigham Young, the Man and His Work.* Salt Lake City: Deseret Book, 1970.

Roberts, B. F. *Comprehensive History of the Church.* Salt Lake City: Deseret News Press. Vol. 4, 1930.

Smith, Jim (son). *Lot Smith's Story, the Echo Canyon War.* Self-published.

Smith, Joseph (with B. H. Roberts). *History of Church.* Salt Lake City: Deseret Book, 1980.

Smith, Lot. Diaries and research compiled by his grandson, Elias, and wife Deanne Craig, Provo, Utah.

Smith, Joseph Fielding. *Essentials in Church History.* Salt Lake City: Deseret Book, 1979.

U.S. Government, Messages and Papers of the Presidents, Washington.

U.S. Government, House Congressional Records and Documents, Washington.

Van Alfen, Nicholas. *Porter Rockwell, Frontier Marshal*, condensed from a master's thesis. Brigham Young University, Provo, Utah 1964.

Wells, Daniel H. Funeral program prepared by his family, 29 March 1891. Brigham Young University Lee Library, Special Collections, Provo, Utah.

Woodruff, Wilford. *Journal*. Compiled by M. F. Cowley. Salt Lake City: Deseret News Press, 1909.

Chapter Eight: Service

EPHRAIM HANKS

"I believe I administered to several hundreds in a single day . . .
[they were] *saved by the power of God."*

Ephraim Hanks could not sleep. A voice kept calling his name. It told him to go—now! Someone needed his help. He left his home in Draper during the middle of the night to ride to church headquarters in Salt Lake City. There, he found a messenger dispatched from President Brigham Young who was looking for him.

Word was received that handcart immigrants were floundering in the snows of Wyoming, freezing and starving to death. Could Elder Hanks be ready in a day or two to look for the missing converts?

Hanks was ready now. He waited only for a blessing from President Young. Then, with a few others, he headed eastward along the Mormon Trail. When storms became particularly ferocious ("I had seen no worse," said Hanks, having weathered many mail runs across the plains), others turned back. It seemed no one could live through such a storm. But Hanks would not be deterred. He pressed on.

When the snow was too deep to continue with his wagon, he unhitched the horses, using one to ride, and loading the other with a makeshift pack. He prayed for buffalo to show, even though all should have long before migrated to wintering grounds. At intervals in the blowing snow, he located two bison and managed to shoot both. He then pressed on until he found the Mormon entourage on the Sweetwater River. The scene before him was as a cemetery with no gravestones. Many were dying; others were about to. Each soul was down to the last four ounces of flour.

They couldn't have been more grateful. Some later wrote with simple poignancy, "A dark spot appeared in the distance. It was . . . Ephraim Hanks!"

Hanks could scarcely believe the misery on display before him: "When I saw the terrible condition of the immigrants on first entering their camp, my heart almost melted within me." He rose up in his saddle, shouting new encouragement. When they saw the buffalo, men, women, and children began eating the meat raw. Most of all they fed on this: more relief parties were on the way.

Hanks regretted he could not save many from loss of feet and fingers due to frostbite. He'd had no formal medical training, yet he spent many hours the first two days halting the spread of infection by removing flesh from bone, and at times, amputating the bone itself. He had learned one thing from years of hardy frontier life: how to face reality squarely. He did what had to be done.

That included spending day and night administering to the sick. The same night he arrived, a woman ran to a nearby tent seeking help for a dying husband. The brother she awakened peered at the woman's ashen husband and declared, "I cannot administer to a dead man." The brother she called on said he needed sleep; he returned to it. Hanks, managing on very little sleep himself in battling snowdrifts to reach the beleaguered Saints, went immediately to work. Determined to save the man's life, he called on several brethren to help him administer to the dying man. They poured consecrated oil over his body. (Hanks never traveled without consecrated oil.) The instant that Hanks concluded praying, he said the man leaped to his feet. The woman rushed outside once more, this time shouting, "My husband was dead but now is alive! Praised be the name of God! The man who brought the buffalo meat has saved him!"

In an interview Hanks gave Andrew Jenson, Latter-day Saint historian, in Wayne County, Utah, June 1891, he took little credit: "I believe I administered to several hundreds in a single day . . . [they were] saved by the power of God."

The suffering handcart Saints could do little to administer to and save themselves. With loved ones dying all around them (one report saying nineteen perished in one night), wolves digging up the buried from shallow graves in sight of loved ones, coupled with various stages of hypo-thermia, the immigrants were both physically and mentally numbed. (As is now known about hypothermia, a lowering of body/brain temperature can alter the power of reasoning.) Hanks's arrival seemed to bring a new level of faith, an iron rod as it were, that the suffering immigrants could grasp. The rescuer remained with the refugees, feeding them buffalo he shot along the way, until they reached Zion.

One man had caused a dramatic turnaround.

When other relief parties arrived from Salt Lake City, the life-saving buffalo rations had nearly run out. Handcarts were now simply aban-doned, as many had grown too rickety and were falling apart due to hasty, late summer preparations at Iowa City, Iowa. The immigrants with their meager belongings eagerly climbed into relief wagons and arrived in Zion 30 November 1858.

The James Willie Handcart Company had arrived about two weeks earlier. In all, the loss of lives from Willie's company was 75 dead of some 400; from Martin's, 150 of 576. A sobered President Young was to later say he would sever from the Church any leader who ever again allowed such tardy departure in crossing the plains. "I will not have such late starts again."

Years later, a man in the Martin Handcart Company who had been given up for dead (no name given by Hanks), was found to be very much alive and well in Cedar City, and then invited Hanks to stop in. He ended up heaping Hanks's wagons with food and farming implements.

This man was only one of many singing praises to Ephraim Hanks. At least two known letters were sent to Hanks and his relatives from those who said they would have surely perished without his help at Martin's Cove.

The above rescue episode was only one example of courageous service in the life of Ephraim Knowlton Hanks. He was described by a non-Mormon, Captain Richard Burton of the English Army, who visited Salt Lake City in 1860, as a "light-haired, good-looking man, a pleasant and humorous countenance . . . touched with the rough cordiality of the mountaineer . . . looking as if . . . to shun neither friend nor foe." Burton's description may have been colored by rumors he had heard in the East that Hanks was a "Mormon desperado," apparently because of the life Hanks lived while delivering mail on the wilderness frontier.

Whatever his physical appearance, the importance of Ephraim Hanks is in his devoted lifetime of service rendered to his Church. As letters written about him attest, he selflessly saved many lives by many different means throughout his earthly sojourn. Hanks administered to a young boy named Thomas at Fort Bridger who got up and walked about after being given up for dead. Hanks's healing hands were also applied to more than one ailing Native American child. Tribal chiefs labeled him a "miracle worker." As a faith-healer among the Native Americans, Hanks was probably equaled only by the legendary "Apostle to the Lamanites," Jacob Hamblin, in southern Utah and northern Arizona.

To understand Hanks's deep devotion to his church, we need to know more about his early life in Ohio and his conversion to the restored gospel. We are indebted in this to a biography of his father by his son Sidney. Hanks was described as a person naturally attracted to the outdoors. He enjoyed hunting and kept the family supplied in squirrel meat. He was also a bit roughshod and undisciplined in his youth. As an adventurous teenage lad, Hanks was eager to see the world. He joined the U. S. Navy for three years. Disobedient on one occasion to military command, he received a number of whiplashes across the back. Obedience to authority suddenly became important to Ephraim Hanks. He had learned a valuable lesson.

After his discharge, Hanks returned home and received a letter from his brother Sydney in Indiana. Sydney wrote that he had "found the true church." Hanks set out immediately to rescue his misguided brother from the Mormons. But partway to Indiana, Hanks got the impression he should return home; there he found that Sydney had come looking for him.

Hanks, and probably Sydney as well, had each been given a dollar from their father's will to buy a copy of the New Testament. Religion was very important in the home. As the two brothers talked late into the night about the Book of Mormon and the restored Church, their mother said she had heard enough. Her idea of religion apparently did not include seeing, let alone conversing, with angels. She invited two Methodist ministers to talk some sense into her sons. Just as Sydney seemed to be getting the best of things, the ministers grew abusive. Hanks ordered them from the house. Their mother objected, instead sending her two sons from the house.

There are no indications from that point on that Hanks or his brother ever looked back. The two traveled to Nauvoo and were baptized just in time to join the Mormon exodus from Nauvoo. In Iowa, Ephraim was one of the first to volunteer for the Mormon Battalion.

After participating in the Battalion's historic march across the continent, Hanks made his way to Utah, ready to settle down and get married. He was greatly disturbed to hear a bishop warn Mormon girls in his flock to watch out for returning Battalion members who would cart off the unsuspecting lasses to California. Hanks confronted the bishop at his home and told him if he persisted in such talk, he, Ephraim Hanks, would take the man's house apart, log by log. There is no indication Hanks did so; but apparently, a frightened bishop ceased his warnings. Hanks courted Harriet Little, a local girl who, like him, loved horses and riding. They were married 22 September 1848.

Ephraim tried farming for a time at a place he called Mountain Dell, east of Salt Lake City (the same name appears on today's maps). When Parley's Canyon was opened up for east-west traffic in 1860, Hanks moved there. But farming on the edge of civilization was too tame for Ephraim Hanks. Athletic in build, and never fearful of physical challenge, Hanks began carrying the mail for President Young from the Great Basin to Missouri's frontier outpost trailhead at St. Joseph. Hanks carried the mail an estimated sixty times, often among Sioux and other tribes on the warpath. Nothing seemed to deter him from getting the mail through. The U. S. Postal Service did not erect any statue to his name, but from accounts given, he was one of the first to exemplify the well-known postal service motto: "Neither snow nor rain nor heat nor gloom of night stays these couriers . . . from their appointed rounds."

Hanks was also selected for the important mission of escorting Dr. John Bernhisel to take his seat in Congress as Utah's first representative to Washington D. C. Bernhisel was not a seasoned frontiersman and, on one occasion, had to be rescued from drowning in the North Platte River. Hanks managed to get his man to the nation's capital safely.

Family accounts say Hanks developed into a man who was disciplined, obedient, spiritually polished, and not one to drink or swear. Yet, he had much to learn about Mormon ways. Sidney, Hanks's son, said in the biography of his father that Hanks once appeared at a dance with a beard and long hair. President Young stepped up and told him to shave it off.

Showing up later, but minus full compliance, President Young sent him back. This time he did as Young requested. The story passed down from generation to generation is that it was given as a test by President Young to determine if the young Ephraim Hanks could follow orders from an ecclesiastical superior. If so, President Young had a work for him to do.

Hanks must have passed, for President Young did, indeed, keep him busy serving the cause of Zion for years to follow.

Another story given by the family is that President Young noted an adobe wall Hanks was building; it was only eight inches thick. Hanks was told by the Mormon leader to take it down and make it twice as thick. When rain poured down later, Hanks became convinced the wall would have washed out if not following President Young's advice. After such experiences, he learned to trust the Mormon leader more fully.

Hanks was also called on for a time to harass Johnston's Army. He managed to sneak in and run off stock, even daring on one occasion to partake of food left out by Army cooks. It was not long, however, before President Young needed Hanks to carry the mail to California. In so doing, Hanks showed savvy and staying power which would surpass western heroes such as Kit Carson and Davy Crockett. Leaving his horses in the vicinity of Carson City, Nevada, due to mounting snowpack, Hanks donned snowshoes to carry the mail with which he had been entrusted across the Sierra Nevada Mountains to San Francisco. Two guides attempted to help him but after two days they ended up where they started. Hanks had to do it alone. He returned within thirty days to see what new assignment President Young might have for him.

In delivering the mail, Hanks had many encounters with Native Americans. He developed a philosophy to never yield to their unjust demands, yet always avoided bloodshed. This treatment was apparently developed when he was called by Mormon leaders to "troubleshoot" among the Goshute tribe in Tooele County. He was sent to kill tribesmen who had been stealing cattle and horses from the settlements. But when Hanks looked down his musket at one of the alleged thieves, his weapon would not fire. Nor would that of any other militia member. In this, Hanks corroborates the testimony of Jacob Hamblin that no one on either side of the skirmish could get their firearms to function. Hanks took it to mean God had other plans for the Lamanites. They must be of some use in his divine plan. Once, two Ute arrows narrowly missed Hanks. Another time, his horse was shot out from under him; two holes showed in his saddle blanket.

Hanks simply refused to quit, whatever the odds, especially if he was on the Lord's errand. His story sometimes reads like fiction. Once when taking a message east for the president of the British Mission, natives stole all he possessed except his clothing and a hidden knife. He managed to sneak close enough to a sleeping adult buffalo cow to cut a hamstring. While his dog drew the animal's attention, he cut the other hamstring, dined on bison meat, and made a robe of the hide. He then found the same tribe which had stolen from him and "stole" back from them two horses so he could continue on his journey.

Twice when captured by Native Americans, according to family accounts, Hanks escaped by pretending to be insane. Talking gibberish and gesturing to the Great Spirit, then rolling and jumping as if possessed, were apparently enough that the natives wanted nothing more to do with him. Once, he dropped a knife in the snow and saw a brave put his foot over it. Hanks pretended not to notice, then lifted his hands to the sky, moving them down to the foot lodged over the knife. He motioned for the Indian to move and retrieved his knife. The natives made way for this man who communed with the Great Spirit.

As Jacob Hamblin had vowed, Hanks was careful to never harm a Lamanite despite some close escapes. He gained a reputation as friend of the natives, some thinking him magic in prophesying buffalo would appear or reappear. Hanks either knew the ways of the bison, or he knew the ways of his Father in Heaven. Whatever, the natives treated this paleface with respect.

In carrying the mail, traveling as lightly as possible, Hanks often had to live off the land. In one account, he made badgers palatable by boiling and reboiling off the strong taste. He sometimes subsisted, like the locals, on rabbits and small animals. He made do with whatever was available. Becoming skilled with a lariat, he once lassoed a young antelope, according to family records. He also shot and lived off bear meat at one time.

Later in life, Hanks did a little prospecting and got lucky. He discovered ore in the Park City region which turned out to be rich in silver and lead. He developed the Green Monster mine, making a good deal of money, but he decided the bawdy mining district was not for him. He moved on.

No longer pressed into service by the Church to run the mail, Hanks retired to a ranch at Burrville near present-day Koosharem. That wasn't wild enough. He settled on Pleasant Creek on the east, or "back side," of what is now Boulder Mountain. Today, the region, bordered by Capitol Reef National Park, is known as Floral Ranch. A natural formation near the ranch shows on highway maps today as "Eph's Tower."

In time, Hanks was raising children and grandchildren along with grain and hay. Occasionally during the winter, he visited the more temperate climate of Cainesville. But given the responsibility of stake patriarch, Hanks spent most of his time at home in Wayne County.

There are various accounts of what Church leaders expected members to do with their plural wives after the Manifesto was issued in 1890. But one thing was for sure: federal government officials began stepping up their hunt for "polygs." Hanks had married three wives, including Thisbe Reed, one of those he had rescued at Martin's Cove. Hanks resolved the "polygamy problem" by sitting down with his wives and deciding he should provide materially for them all, yet live with only one, Thisbe. The other two agreed to divorce, at least as far as the law of the land might show. Thus, when federal marshals visited him in the early 1890s seeking to earn a $50 reward for turning in (and convicting) a Mormon co-habitater, all they got was a nice visit with Hanks, one wife, and his "friends."

In his late sixties, Hanks took the Mormon mail east one last time, by train. He died at age seventy on 9 June 1896. His funeral and burial in Cainesville were described by newspaper accounts as a rather cheerful affair. "O death where is thy sting? O grave where is thy victory?" wrote a reporter for a Salt Lake City newspaper. After all, what had Ephraim Knowlton Hanks, or his posterity, to seriously regret after a life of such dedicated service?

NOTES

Berrett, William E. *The Restored Church*. Salt Lake City: Deseret Book, 1949.

"Ephraim Hanks: Hero." *Contributor Magazine*. The Church of Jesus Christ of Latter-day Saints, 14:202–205.

Hanks, Sidney and E. K. Hanks. *Scouting for the Mormons on the Great Frontier, including interview with Andrew Jenson, June, 1891.* Salt Lake City: Deseret Book, 1948;

Brigham Young University Lee Library, Special Collections, Provo, Utah.

Roberts, B. H., Comp. *History of Church*. With reference to Richard Burton's *City of the Saints*, pp. 191–2.

Wixom, Hartt, Hamblin. *A Modern Look at the Frontier Life and Legend of Jacob Hamblin*. Springville: Cedar Fort, 1996.

Chapter Nine: Loyalty
SOLOMON WIXOM

"The worst you can do is kill me, and I can stand that."

As a new Latter-day Saint convert, Solomon Wixom could have escaped mob persecution by simply remaining where he was in central Illinois, but his brethren across the border in Caldwell County were in trouble. What had been mere "excitement" was suddenly growing dangerously hostile. Missouri mobsters weren't just telling Mormons to get out. They were enforcing it with guns.

Although he knew little about his new church, Solomon knew he had to go and help his new friends. In so doing, he not only joined the Battle of Crooked River but was an eyewitness to the death of beloved Apostle David W. Patten, the first Mormon martyr to fall at hands of the Missouri mobsters.

Solomon is described as "rather tall, spare of build, thin face and blue eyes." He was an "immovable man once making up his mind . . . if he undertook a task of any kind, he completed it." At age twenty-two, he listened to the Mormon missionaries, liked what he heard, and was baptized into The Church of Jesus Christ of Latter-day Saints in 1832 by Lyman Wight. (For more about Lyman Wight, see chapter two.) Solomon carried no firearms or other weapons; he carried only a courageous motto recorded in his diary: "The worst you can do is kill me, and I can stand that. No, I am not afraid of you."

Although Solomon was overtaken by the "ague" (most likely the flu), he "prayed to the Lord to give me strength to help in defending His cause and His people. I was healed by the power of the God of Israel, so I went forth with the Army of Israel."

Near "Adamonda Ahmoan," as Solomon spelled it in his journal (Adam Ondi Ahman, where Joseph Smith said Adam and Eve lived in the Garden of Eden), Solomon witnessed a solemn pledge by Joseph and records it as "proclaiming with a loud voice to all Israel, 'I have drawn my sword from its sheath and I swear by the living God that it shall never return again 'till I can go and be treated by others as they wish to be treated by me,' and all the army said, 'Amen.'"

But the desire of Joseph's heart for peace was not soon in coming. Solomon describes the tragic battle of Crooked River (in southwest Caldwell County) in these words: "The mob kept gathering and driving the Saints from the out settlements to Far West and Diaham [Adam Ondi Ahman] 'till they had destroyed all their houses, farms. . . . On hearing that they had taken some of our brethren prisoners and were miserably treating them and had camped on Crooked River, David W. Patten, one of the Twelve Apostles, called out a company of Saints and went to rescue them from the mob which he did, and in the noble act, he laid down his life. He fell close to my side." Solomon records that Patten was ambushed by a retreating mobber hiding behind a tree. David died later that evening from his wounds. The date given by Solomon: 25 October 1838.

Patten died with these words on his lips, according to Drusilla Hendricks, whose husband was seriously wounded nearby, "Ann, don't weep. I have kept the faith. I have finished my course . . . whatever you do else, O do not deny the faith." (See *Women's Voices*, p. 91.)

Solomon's account says that as Patten fell, he uttered the words "God and Liberty" and bid the little band of brethren to continue the charge. The riffraff fled in all directions, "for thereby the prisoners were rescued. We returned to Far West but four of our men were slain." Times were indeed perilous, for the following Tuesday, seventeen Mormon men were slaughtered and many others wounded by a barbaric mob at Haun's Mill a few miles from Far West.

Joseph Smith was to record later in the Doctrine and Covenants, 124:19 and 130: "David Patten I have taken unto myself; behold his priesthood no man taketh from him . . . My servant David Patten's with me at this time." The precise place where Patten is buried (somewhere in or near Far West) is not known. Some graves were discovered in modern times by historians searching the abandoned Far West Mormon cemeteries; but Patten's was not one of those located.

Apostle Patten certainly deserves the title "loyal." He had temporarily aligned himself with the Methodists but told friends "there is no true religion on Earth." He believed, however, that Christ's church would be established in his lifetime. When learning of the teachings of Joseph Smith, Patten immediately embraced the Mormon faith. He served missions in Michigan, New York, Maine, Vermont, Canada, and to the Southern States. On 15 February 1835, he was ordained to the apostleship. While in Tennessee, Patten was arrested for promising the Holy Ghost to those who were baptized. He responded by telling the judge that his courtroom was full of wicked men; to which the judge replied that Patten "must have secret weapons to speak with such courage." David replied, according to family annals, "I have weapons you know not of and they are given me of God."

Upon learning of the Saints' suffering in Missouri, Patten could not remove the plight of those poor souls from his mind. He arrived in Jackson County in 1833 at about the time his fellow churchmen were being expelled. Unflinchingly, he joined the effort at Crooked River to help them, as Solomon attests.

Solomon also remained incredibly loyal to his church throughout many trials in Missouri. He helped dig the foundation of the temple in Far West at a time when the enemy prowled about looking for Mormons. He was also instrumental in many priesthood healings, as recorded in his diary. Continues Solomon: "In a few days the whole country was in arms. The mob under cover of the law [Governor Lilburn Boggs's infamous extermination order having been issued 27 October 1838] near Far West, pitched their camp on Goose Creek, and surrounded the dwelling place where Bro. Shaver used to live. There were at that time 5 or 6 women living in it. Among them was my wife Sarah and child of only two years old. My wife was then almost to deliver her second child. On or about the last of October, the heads of the church were given up to the hands of the mob by Colonel Hinkle, the city of Far West was to be given up and the next day I had an interview with Bro. Hiram [sic] Smith . . . he advised me to leave the state forthwith."

Solomon sent for his wife, "had a short interview with her, told her the counsel I had received. She said, 'go, make your escape, leave me in the hand of the Lord and the brethren.' I took leave of her and the young child, not knowing that I should ever see them again but I knew they were in the hands of an all-wise Providence."

There was no time to make or find a wagon to carry family members, even if Sarah could withstand such a journey in her condition. She would remain behind until the baby was born. Solomon, with several other priesthood-holders, including "Dimic [*sic*] Huntington" and some others whose names Solomon "had forgotten," fled north and east across the Grand River. Ironically, they felt safe when reaching Indian country. In a few days, they reached Illinois and were soon among Solomon's wife's people.

Solomon arranged for a man named Green Butterfield to return and get his wife and new son, who was born near Far West. "In the month of Feb. he brought them to her father's house. . . . The Lord brought us together again; although we were robbed of almost everything we had of an earthly nature yet we felt rich and happy that our lives were spared 'till we met again."

Ever since Boggs's Extermination Order drove the Saints from Missouri, Latter-day Saint readers have understandably felt great sympathy and sorrow for those pioneers who put their cause above their own physical welfare. But from Solomon's writings, it would appear he spent no time feeling sorry for himself. He and his peers seemed buoyed up, despite afflictions, by a spiritual strength surpassing the understanding of those who were not there.

Solomon kept busy preaching the word of God, comforting the few scattered Saints, and telling them that God would soon gather His people again. "The Lord gave me His holy spirit and I was blessed much in preaching to the people; gainsayers were confounded. We had a small branch of the church called Crooked Creek [remembering the site where David Patten fell]. We met often and called on the name of the Lord in behalf of the Saints in prison [including Joseph and Hyrum Smith in Liberty Jail] and the cause of Zion. In this way we got along rejoicing in the Lord our God."

Solomon often confronted Methodist ministers in front of their own congregations. On one occasion, a minister opposed Solomon's discourse with considerable malice, "in the most abusive language stated that I was an impostor and for proof of the same, brought up paper of the day concerning Jo [*sic*] Smith and rallied against the Book of Mormon and against the ordinances of the gospel, saying they were not essential to salvation." Solomon concluded that the people became disgusted with the minister, "so all became confusion . . . and the meeting closed."

The next day, a Methodist minister (apparently not the same one) challenged Solomon to a spiritual debate and promised to occupy only two hours. He took four. Taking so long to relinquish the pulpit, as Solomon put it, "The people became weary and dissatisfied at his proceedings and the most of them went away before he finished his lingo of stuff. I then arose . . . but for the want of time I could not say much."

But that night by candlelight, Solomon preached to a large returning audience, "and to the astonishment of all present and by assistance of the spirit of God, made the former discourse [by the Methodist minister] look black, which was its true color . . . the people were very attentive until I was through . . . I baptized James Howard, notwithstanding the opposition and power of darkness which appeared to prevail." A short time later, the Mormon missionary also baptized and confirmed four more souls, including Sarah Avery, who would become his wife.

Solomon would not back off despite what he termed "black" opposition. The energized Mormon missionary assisted with many faith healings, including one in behalf of a boy scalded "very bad." Solomon laid hands on the boy's head and "the fire came out." In the morning, the child was "perfectly well." Several others in the same household were healed by the elder's laying on of hands. One child had lost use of her arm; the other "had never been well from the womb. They both recovered immediately to the astonishment of all who knew the circumstances, this affected by the prayer of faith and the laying on of hands in the name of the Lord."

Solomon includes one sentence about the temple in Caldwell County: "I attended the meeting at Far West and helped dig the foundation of the temple at Far West." This temple, of course, has not yet been built, although the Lord decreed in Doctrine and Covenants 115:7–12 that the site constituted "holy ground." Verse twelve specifically says of this temple, "Let them . . . labor diligently until it shall be finished."

The Church of Jesus Christ of Latter-day Saints still owns the Far West temple lot site (unlike the site in Independence, which is owned by the followers of Granville Hedrek, or the Hedrekites). But after the temple cornerstones were laid, armed backwoodsmen stood watch to prevent further work.

Some opposition to the Mormons, already under siege from without, came from members themselves. Solomon was accused by a brother John Lemmon in church court of "breaking the law of the land." Presiding at the court was Thomas B. Marsh, president of the Council of the Twelve, who dismissed the case (no details given) and held the accuser to be at fault. Lemmon's response was ruled to be insubordinate and in contempt. Solomon's accuser was then "cut off from the church," according to Solomon's diary.

Solomon considered such incidents as "having a stumpy row of corn to hoe." As a boy, his older brothers would tease him in the fields about falling behind in his weeding. Solomon answered that it was because they had given him the "stumpy row to hoe." The stumpy rows would continue; but Solomon wrote that he "liked" hardships and privations. They were the means of growth.

Solomon and Sarah found temporary peace and contentment in moving to a new home in Illinois, some forty miles southeast of Carthage. Soon, however, they began to hear "rumors of trouble" in Nauvoo, where most of the other members had settled. "There were all sorts of reports in circulation. The brethren would often ask what it would amount to. I told them I did not know but to be still and attend to their own business and pray much and be humble and the Lord would bring all things right."

Yet "things" grew worse. "Along in the month of June the excitement reached high. Our business was threatened and it seemed we were in danger. Orders were given to the Schuyler County military unit (including a handful of Mormons in the area) to have their men in readiness to march to Carthage if necessary." The military that "should be ready to march" was ordered by Governor Thomas Ford to quell any uprising from the Mormons in Nauvoo.

Thus, with considerable irony, Solomon and fellow Mormons were expected to march against Mormons. It caused a huge dilemma for Solomon. "On the 23rd or 24th of June we were all notified to be on the parade ground armed and equipped according to law. I visited the brethren, told them it was best to go, so they came out and went with the militia. I took a yoke of oxen and wagon to carry the baggage."

Solomon managed a concession from his military commander for himself and Church brethren: "I obtained a pledge from Capt. Briant Brown that he would not let his men abuse us inasmuch as we belonged to his company and were under his charge. We arrived in Carthage on the 25th of June, stayed there 'till the 27th. In the time we were there we saw the prisoners marched to the courthouse in midst of cursing and swearing of the multitude, some spitting at them, some threatening their lives. They looked like devils in human form."

This eye-witness account is one of few given at Carthage immediately prior to the impending martyrdom. Solomon would witness it at close range because he was a member of the Illinois militia.

Apparently, security officers (Governor Ford had left Carthage at that time) no longer feared an insurrection among friends of the prisoners, Joseph and Hyrum Smith, Willard Richards, and John Taylor. No large contingent of Mormons hovered near in an attempt to free the four inmates. Thus, Solomon's company was dismissed by the militia commander to return home.

As they did, one Benjamin West took umbrage to those in the company friendly to the Mormons; they were "as bad as the Mormons. This raised an excitement in the camp and to make it still worse they had a bottle of whisky along. When we got about six miles from Carthage the row began between the said West and a man by the name of James Lynn. They were both in the wagon; Lynn jumped onto West, pounded him, tore his eyes half out of his head; finally, the oxen got frightened and stampeded, and before the men could part them, West . . . fell in the ditch he dug for his neighbor."

After stopping for the night, "All went to bed quiet and nice, but I could not sleep. My mind was in trouble. There was none to free my mind. If at any time they saw 2 of us [Mormons] talking together they were jealous of us, so I lay in deep thought . . . what will they do with our brethren in prison?"

The men lay still until about ten o' clock when they heard the distant sound of a horse on the gallop. "It came nearer and nearer. I thought what does this mean? Soon it came to the door, a man's voice was heard rather in an excited tone. 'Ho! Lo!' I arose, opened the door. 'What is the matter?'

"'Joseph and Hiram [*sic*] are killed!'

Several blank pages follow. One can surmise that Solomon did not like writing any more on such a subject, or perhaps that what was said wasn't polite English. Possibly, the page was ripped out and thrown away.

Yet, the message is essentially there. Solomon and his peers feared the worst and it happened. The Mormon leaders were murdered without trial. The account of a mob breaking in to shoot Joseph and Hyrum and wounding John Taylor, Willard Richards being unhurt, as the Carthage "guards" yielded to the mob, is well known and detailed in *History of the Church* 7:31. But Solomon's account adds many insights.

After a period of deep mourning, Solomon joined the exodus from Nauvoo, stopping in Council Bluffs, Iowa, where he could be most useful, helping to build shelters for the emigrants on their way west. He writes that another village was built on the Nebraska side of the Missouri River, called Winter Quarters. Solomon stayed here for three years to assist the Saints with his skills of carpentry and woodwork. He married a second wife, Harriett Teeples, on 15 January 1846. The following year she bore her husband a son. But when she decided to continue west, Solomon determined he must stay with Sarah who was too ill to travel. The couple remained in Winter Quarters with their two sons, Justin Chauncey and Solomon Avery (see chapter one for more of his story), for another year to watch over Sarah. Despite such close attention, Sarah passed away.

To his surprise, when Solomon arrived in Zion, he found that his wife had somehow obtained a church divorce, and was remarried to David Sessions. Her infant son by Solomon, Seth, had been rechristened "James Monroe Sessions."

For nearly three quarters of a century, the two families lost track of one another. Solomon lived for a time in the Cottonwood area of Salt Lake Valley where he married Hannah Montgomery. Later, they moved to Brigham City, where he prospered raising cattle. He bought a coffee mill, converted it to mill grain and corn, and in so doing "was able to feed many hungry mouths." Solomon was most content in this new home. Nevertheless, he was loyal to President Brigham Young's call to settle the cold, rugged Bear Lake country in what was then Utah; it became part of Idaho in 1890 when the Idaho was granted statehood.

Solomon used his carpentry skills as before, to build up a new community in and around Paris, Bloomington, and Liberty. In his old age, he was described as tall, spare of build, with a thin face and blue eyes, and light brown hair, curly but thin.

Hannah became known as an excellent cook, with her children saying of her, "She could make a banquet out of nothing." Friends wrote that her home, like that of many other pioneer women, "was made lovely by the use of quick, efficient hands, which were never idle during her waking hours. The beautiful quilts, rugs, embroidery work, were masterpieces of art."

Her husband gained a reputation as a lover of children, who told them many stories, riddles, and jokes. By now, he had nineteen of his own who could be in the family audience. Solomon might have had more children but one wife, Catherine, separated from him. As Solomon's descendants J. H. Wixom and Ruth Widdison put it, "Solomon wasn't really much of a polygamist, for twice was he possessed of a plural wife . . . both quit him early in the game."

Being separated from the main body of Saints in Salt Lake Valley, and in another state, Solomon never again saw his son James Monroe. Solomon died 1 March 1879 in Paris, Idaho. Not until 1921 did the family circle, including descendants of Solomon and Harriett, finally gather to meet with James. By then, "long lost" James (Wixom, Sessions) was seventy-six. Through it all, though, Solomon Wixom remained loyal not only to his family and his church, but also himself.

Notes

Black, Susan Easton. *Who's Who in the Doctrine and Covenants.* Salt Lake City: Bookcraft, 1997.

The Doctrine and Covenants. Salt Lake City: The Church of Jesus Christ of Latter-day Saints, 1987.

Egbert, Carol. Family papers and personal interview. Layton, Utah, 18 February 2000.

Godfrey, Kenneth W., Audrey M. Godfrey, and Jill Mulvay Derr. *Women's Voices: An Untold History of the Latter-day Saints 1830–1900.* Salt Lake City: Deseret Book, 1982.

Wilson, Lycurgus A. *Life of David Patten, First Apostolic Martyr.* Peoria: Eborn Books, 1992.

Wixom, Solomon, Diary. In possession of family members.

Wixom, J. H. and Ruth S. Widdison. *Wixom Family History.* Salt Lke City: Publishers Press, 1963.

Chapter Ten: Courage

SABINA SCHEIB

"She now lived in a one-room hovel . . . a happy woman."

In the mid-1800s London was a city of culture and refinement, at least for those who had money and education. It was also the headquarters of what the English considered a superior way of life. Historians were fond of saying, "The sun never sets on the British Empire."

Most of the world knew about the dominance of the British Navy and the acute intellectual and organizational skills of its people which ruled Canada, India, Australia, much of South Africa, and at one time the new land known as the United States.

However, for the majority of the population, little was known about England in America, save that two wars had been fought between the countries. Americans had won the Revolutionary War under the leadership of George Washington and had repelled the British in the War of 1812, although the British first succeeded in capturing and partially burning the American's new capital at Washington D. C. For some Americans, their greatest exposure to their former mother country was through the eloquent wit of Shakespeare and Sir Arthur Conan Doyle's mystery stories about detective Sherlock Holmes.

England was, however, a fertile proselyting ground for the Mormon missionaries. Hundreds of elders who found many converts were sent to England in the mid-1800s. But for there new converts to gather the money needed to sail to the unknown in America was something else. An elder might experience a certain feeling of chaos standing in London's historic Hyde Park, preaching that God had recently revealed Himself to an obscure fourteen-year-old American boy named Joseph Smith in the state of New York, and then expecting that those hearing this word should leave the comfort and security of England for a journey of six to eight weeks across the ocean.

At the same time, those who had lived under the dominant discipline of the Church of England—the same denomination which had ostensibly come about so that King Henry VIII could gain a divorce—might well be hungry for religious truth. After all, it was for such reasons the Pilgrims and Puritans of a few centuries before had fled to America. America was the land of religious opportunity, was it not? To give up all they knew, based on a young man's preaching, amid an army of hecklers in a public park? Was this the will of God?

That was the question John and Catherina Scheib pondered in the late 1840s. Should they as wise parents subject their large family and elite lifestyle to break from servants and maids and private lessons and sophisticated grand balls to leave all they knew—for the promise of a Mormon Zion in America? On the high seas or during perilous travel by wagon across a wilderness filled with savages and wild beasts would their children say that they had made a terrible mistake? Could they forgive their parents attempt to do the right thing for them?

It required some time before the Scheibs could make such a monumental decision. John was a skilled piano maker with a renowned reputation with the Erard Piano Company which had won first prize at the Great Exhibition at the Crystal Palace in Paris, France, in 1851. It was known as "the prize of all the world." John's artistic craftsmanship had made him a wealthy man. The family was held in high esteem by people in high places. Government officials dropped over for tea in the afternoon. With a reputation for fine breeding and culture, they moved in London's highest social circles. Their Victorian way of life was the envy of many. Moving would only jeopardize all John had worked for. Catherina was educated, cultured, refined, and descended from nobility through the line of Ann Moravia, vintage 1740. Blood lines were more than a pedigree in old England. They were assurance of respect from the elite.

Their daughter Sabina was a product of her heritage and enjoyed many educational advantages. Nearby was the birthplace of William Shakespeare. In London resided some of the world's great museums of art. The

Scheibs' daily routine was filled with learning in the fields of science and academic pursuits at the hallowed University of London. Sabina could receive the same education as her mother. Photographs of her reflect a woman of petite features, with dark hair, dark eyes, and with an elegant, confident bearing, suggestive of one raised with the finer things of life.

Yet, some years following the family's decision to give it all up and sail to America, Sabina would call home a one-room hovel with a dirt roof, children playing on straw floors, no fixed doors or windows to hold out winter temperatures plummeting to thirty and forty degrees below zero. Sabina's grandson Edward L. Hart said of her home in Blooming-ton, Idaho, that it was "so cold even the native Shoshone people spent their winters elsewhere." There were no museums of art or cultural refine-ments around the corner, no universities. Yet, a granddaughter of Sabina's described her as an unmurmering and happy woman.

How so? To understand it, we need to explore Sabina's goals in life. Much of her story is told by grandsons, one of them Edward L. Hart, a grandson who lived in the same environment in Bear Lake County, Idaho, where Sabina raised most of her nine children. In an interview with Edward in Provo, Utah, 2 March 2000, he said that much of his determi-nation to gain an education at Oxford and a PhD in philosophy, plus years of distinguished, award-winning teaching at Brigham Young University, came about because of the influence of his nurturing grandmother.

All of Sabina's sons and daughters would pursue education beyond high school, an extremely rare thing in those days. Three sons became prominent lawyers.

No monument or pedestal was ever raised to the name of Sabina Scheib other than her modest burial marker in Idaho, as a plural wife of James H. Hart, for years the Church's immigration agent in New York City. Sabina is not even mentioned in the great biographies written of promi-nent Mormon women, including historian Kate Carter's *Our Pioneer Her-itage*, nor *Women's Voices* by three prominent Latter-day Saint historians. Her life was in many ways, an obscure life behind the walls of her own home. The same might be said of many faithful pioneer women, modest and unassuming, who made few waves known to the world or even their own church. Unfortunately, they seem forgotten today.

According to her son Alfred A. Hart, Sabina didn't want to be bap-tized when turning eight years of age. "She was somewhat indifferent. But one night she had a dream, a remarkable manifestation, which convinced her conclusively of the need for this sacred ordinance. It was immediately performed." Some time later, her faith was kindled "by witnessing a miracle in the restoration to health and strength of her sister, Annie, age 10."

It happened this way, according to a granddaughter, Adina Lloyd: "Annie had the disease called 'consumption' [now known as tuberculosis]. When the doctor came to see her . . . he said that one lung was completely gone and the other almost gone; she could not live through the night." Of that he was certain.

"Lorenzo Snow who was serving in England . . . accepted John Scheib's invitation to go home with him for dinner after a church meeting. John explained Annie's sickness on the way home. Snow said he would like to administer to the little sick girl before sitting down to dinner. He promised Annie that she would live to come to Zion and receive her endowments. The family sat down for dinner. In a few minutes Annie came to the table saying she wanted to eat with them . . .

"The next day the doctor passed the house expecting to see a black wreath on the door . . . not seeing the wreath [of death] the doctor came into the house and was startled to see Annie playing noisily with her brothers and sisters. Upon examination, he found no signs of the disease; both lungs were normal. He called her a 'Little Resurrection.'"

According to family members, this event had a profound impact on Sabina that she never forgot. It seemed that her faith in the Lord and the elders of The Church of Jesus Christ of Latter-day Saints never wavered after that remarkable experience. Said son Alfred at a later date: "She was a woman of remarkable faith in the Lord. She had implicit faith in Him."

She would need it for what lay ahead. In Sabina's brief, four-page journal, she explains that on the date following her father's piano triumph in the Great Exhibition, 10 January 1852, the family sailed for America. Her father had previously ventured onto sailing vessels and became seriously seasick. Nevertheless, he consented to cross the ocean that his family might find a home with the Saints of God in Zion.

John and Catherina would suffer other hardships. All nine of Sabina's brothers and sisters died before reaching their 21st birthday. One family history says that most of them succumbed "through exposure and contagion incident to hardships in crossing the ocean and the plains to Salt Lake City." Actually, only one did die while actually en route, nine-month-old Pierre. He was buried at sea near Cuba after contracting what was probably pneumonia. One history says the "ship's doctor worked hard but couldn't save his life." Several siblings died at a very early age of scarlet fever after reaching Salt Lake City. Anna Maria, 18, ended up dying of typhus in Salt Lake City. John or Catherina may well have lamented leaving behind familiar family physicians in England for those in a strange and newly settled land. Yet, there is no evidence of them ever murmuring or complaining about their decision to join with members of their new faith in Zion.

Says one family history, "They left behind many sorrowing friends and relatives whom they never saw in this life again." They sailed across the ocean on a ship named Kennebec, then to New Orleans, and then up the Mississippi on the steamer Pride of the West.

Of time spent on the Atlantic Ocean, perhaps some insight might be gained of the perils and difficulties in such travel, and indeed the faith required to endure it, by reading *Our Mayflower Ancestors and Their Descendants* by Sabina's granddaughter, Jocelyn Faux. The book poses this question: "Who Would Sail with the Pilgrims—Would You? Imagine being squeezed into a 90-foot long boat with 101 other members, one third of whom were children, plus a crew of 25. They had to put their faith in Captain Christopher Jones to guide them by sun and stars . . . it was not easy to forego privacy for 65 days of travel. The only chance to wash was when the waves washed overboard and soaked them, and there was no chance to dry until the sun shone again . . . the surly, suspicious crew did not help matters. One can imagine how the crew felt about the psalm-singing and prayers of such a peculiar and foolhardy group!"

Of course, the *Kennebec* came along well after the Mayflower of 6 September 1620. The former undoubtedly was more seaworthy and perhaps larger. But in sailing for New Orleans, the *Kennebec* had much farther to go than the *Mayflower* which landed at Cape Cod, Massachusetts. The *Mayflower* also had contained a homogeneous group of pilgrims who could have things more their own way on a chartered ship than the Scheibs and a handful of Mormons who must have been viewed as a most peculiar minority on the *Kennebec*.

Yet, there are also parallels in the two expeditions, for all suffered from restricted space; all were at the mercy of a captain and crew of which passengers knew little; the very vessel beneath their feet and over their heads shook with each day's storm lashing out new violence. The Latter-day Saints said prayers and quoted their many scriptures as did the pilgrims. But the followers of Joseph Smith may have seemed even more odd quoting from something called the Book of Mormon rather than the Bible.

The following contains Sabina's account (with her punctuation) of the family's trek after setting foot on land. "Waited six weeks there [Kanesville] for the Wagons to be made. The material for the wagons was destroyed, being on the Saluda that was blown up on April, 1852. The wagons, when finished, we started to cross the plains in the St. Louis Company. Captain McGraw over 50 wagons, Captain Burnet over our ten, every ten Wagons had other Captains. We arrived in Great Salt Lake City, September the 20th, 1852. After camping in our Wagon 2 days, Father Bought a House of Mr. Thomas Grey . . . Father built a large house close to the one he bought. He lived in that house till he died, 16 February 1886 . . . all testifying to his goodness, kindness, faithfulness, integrity and unassuming character."

Sabina says nothing of the trek itself across the prairies of Iowa, Nebraska, and Wyoming into the Rocky Mountains of Utah. It is known that the family traveled in three wagons pulled by six horses. There must have been many challenges for a London-raised family in a frontier environment. But whatever they encountered was apparently overcome by mustering forth another dose of faith and grit. The family's arrival in September indicates that despite a six-week delay in obtaining wagons, the departure from Kanesville was early enough to escape much of the snow and cold suffered by other companies which left later.

It had been eight months since leaving England. With his piano-making skills, John helped build the now-famous tabernacle organ which has enriched the lives of conference goers for more than a hundred years on Temple Square.

Several years after their arrival in Zion, and living in a large home, the Scheibs began inviting conference visitors to their home for dinner and to stay overnight. They enjoyed extending hospitality to others, whether they knew them or not. In October of 1855, they allowed Anna to remain home from conference to prepare a meal for these visitors. When they arrived home, they found the table set and ready for dinner and food on the stove to keep warm. Sadly, they also found her lying on her bed wearing her white temple clothes; she was dead.

Reading about such events from pioneer times 150 years later, one may fail to fully grasp the tragedy. For those like the Scheibs, it might have been worse because they would be tempted to wonder what if they had never departed home for an unknown frontier.

Now only Sabina and Elizabeth of the Scheib children were left. Jacob had died in 1854 of scarlet fever. John had no one carry on the family name. Elizabeth was also soon to die. She loved horseback riding with her own beautiful saddle and bridle. Sometimes with friends she rode all over the valley, jumping barriers or racing. One day after returning from a ride, she felt hot and flushed. She poured water on her head from a pump at side of the house to cool off. The next day she awoke with a high temperature. When the fever did finally subside, she was left with the mind of a young child, according to a family account. She lived about a year longer. Her family wondered if the sudden cold water on her feverish body had done the damage. Speculation later was that she had died of meningitis. With the death, Catherina and her one remaining daughter, Sabina, became closer than ever. Catherina would cling dearly to Sabina, her last child.

Sabina told friends she could never marry into polygamy. Yet, she was smitten by a tall, handsome lawyer named James H. Hart, who was also a convert from England. He was thirty-four, she was twenty-one. Sabina married him even though he had earlier taken Emily Ellingham to wife.

When James was called in 1865 to lay out the town of Bloomington in the remote Bear Lake country of Idaho, it proved a task Sabina could never have fathomed in her childhood. It also proved one more challenge for Catherina. She felt so lonely that she asked Sabina to let three-year-old Anna come live with her. Sabina promised she would do so when Anna was ten.

Idaho wilderness or no, Sabina determined to adjust to this new environment, bringing culture to her children and reading them good books at every opportunity. She would instill within them a love for both the restored gospel and fine literature. According to her son Alfred, Sabina was conversant with the writings of Charles Dickens, Walter Scott, George Eliot, and William Shakespeare. "She had a remarkable memory and could share with her children all that she had read while growing up. It was of great value to them."

Sabina was, of course, under a great responsibility for the health of her children; there was no physician closer than Logan, Utah, through a mountain pass some 75 miles away and closed to all travel during the winter. If the children got sick, she "gave them a drink of water and said a prayer," according to Alfred. "She made the Lord a particular friend and drew near to Him day and night, in which she felt a divine sense of security."

Alfred wrote: "Her four sons all served missions . . . were greatly honored by receiving high callings in the priesthood [the oldest, Charles H. was sustained a member of the First Council of Seventy] . . . they could each say, as Lincoln said, 'All that I am, all that I ever hope to be, I owe to my angel mother.'"

Sabina was a woman who treasured her children to such an extent that she was prone to worry much about them. One night, three of them decided to sleep in a haystack without telling her. They explained it the next day, but unable to sleep until all were home safely, Mother went looking for them, calling each by name. Feeling guilty, they finally turned themselves in to their detective mother and hurried home.

By the time Anna was ten, Catherina had passed away. Before long, Anna died of a heart condition. Sabina grieved and could not be comforted. Then her mother came to her in a dream and said, "Have you forgotten your promise? You said Anna could come to live with me when she was 10."

Sabina had acquired the habit of drinking tea in the afternoon in England, and she worked hard to get over this Word of Wisdom breach. She had other challenges as well. One day she found a Shoshone brave at her door (the opening then covered only by a quilt, the windows by a shawl) and quickly gave him biscuits and flour. She sighed in relief when he went away. According to Edward Hart (*Mormon in Motion*, p. 176, this was none other than Chief Washakie, who became such a fast friend of the Mormon settlements.) Sabina had to carry water almost daily and often cut and carry firewood before any of her children were old enough to help. She found prayer a daily, sometimes hourly, ritual.

As a second wife, Sabina records no complaints; but she became a special trial to Emily. Emily had been the only wife of James H. for nine years before Sabina came along, and kept a journal in 1862 indicating some serious problems. Life in the new polygamous triangle was most trying during the first year and a half. Emily's journal provides many insights into just how difficult polygamy could be, even with two devoted Latter-day Saint women determined to live it successfully.

To understand Emily's dilemma, let us take a closer look at the situation. She was four years older than James, forty to his thirty-six. Sabina was twenty-two, and described as not only much younger than Emily but "strong-willed and attractive." Emily joined the faith after being a confirmed invalid all of her life. Agreeing to baptism, she was carried to the water. Following baptism, she took her first steps and was strong in step for the remainder of her life. Her husband referred to this as "a miracle." The doctors "had given her up as 'incurable . . . she was healed by the power of God.'"

When Emily's family emigrated from Wales, it involved much soul-searching, just as it had for Sabina. According to Emily, her faith was sorely tested; she felt that her husband's once total affection for her was now being diluted by Sabina. Emily wrote of a "bitter trial, to me worse than death." She prayed for the Lord to "stand by me . . . and I will bless and praise thy name for ever and ever, Amen."

Emily wrote that she felt Sabina took up too much of her husband's time and failed to show his first wife the proper respect. One entry reads as James leaves for Salt Lake City where Sabina then lived, "He ought to be more kind and loving to me for the sacrifice I have made . . . he promised to stand me and help me bear it."

Of course, neither woman had any prior experience at being a plural wife. There were domestic problems. Emily had been given a spinning wheel. But then Sabina received one as well—wasn't one spinning wheel in the family enough? Yet, they worked at their problem until Edward and Alfred could say, "Aunts Emily and Sabina [in Mormondom at that time a plural wife was either grandmother or aunt] . . . became near and dear friends. Their souls were knit together in the bonds of love and friendship which deepened as the years rolled by."

The two finally worked things out to the point that when anything affected either's life, one hurried to tell the other. Emily shared with Sabina the knowledge she gained through the grapevine that federal "polyg" hunting marshals were after their husband. They caught him at his office once, but James managed to give the marshal the slip by stepping out the back door as the marshal stepped through the front door. Such prosecution of their husband was to continually bring the two wives together. Instead of remaining rivals, they bonded, dealing with common hardships.

One factor which probably helped their relationship was that their husband was gone so much as the Church Emigration Agent to St. Louis and New York; James H. also made a trip to Paris, France, where he had served a mission. These absences meant that his wives needed one another if for no other reason than to commiserate that they rarely saw their husband.

Emily died in May 1892, at the age of sixty-five. Her life had, indeed, been a trial, not only because of polygamy but because she lost five of her six children, born prematurely, shortly after birth. She was remembered as one who had seen much affliction in living the gospel but through it all was "true to her friends, her religion, her God." Most important: she and Sabina had made their peace.

But Sabina would soon find herself in Emily's place as first wife. James H. married another wife, Lizzie, a young and very pretty woman. Sabina told family members that James made one major mistake in their relationship. He not only married Lizzie without telling Sabina, but at a time when Sabina was in bed recovering from childbirth. Sabina had been sick for several days and knew she looked it.

Things were further strained when James gave Liz the same amount of money as Sabina, who had to spend hers on the children. Liz could spend hers on fine clothes or whatever she wanted. Sabina's granddaughter Adina said Sabina found it difficult, if not impossible, to forgive her husband for this breach of etiquette, and most particularly for marrying Liz without her consent and bringing her in for introductions when she, Sabina, looked so pale and sick. It became a double tragedy for Sabina when her newborn child died shortly after birth.

Liz was also a convert from the British Isles and when writing her history late in life, concluded with this statement: "In these labors and associations among the daughters of Zion and the noble mothers of Israel, they have afforded the greatest happiness that I have experienced during my life." She seemed to feel no strain in being a polygamous wife.

In 1904 a tragic accident changed the lives of all three in this polygamous marriage. Lizzie was killed in an accident which severely injured James. After visiting relatives in Montpelier, Idaho, James's spirited horses turned so sharply at the Ovid Creek Bridge that the sleigh fell into the ravine, dragging with it both horses and occupants. It was believed Lizzie died instantly.

Family members say Liz's sister did not recognize the principle of plural marriage and remained home from Liz's funeral to remove her house of all furnishings, including the carpet and drapes. James H. and family did not contest it "to avoid notoriety and adverse publicity."

Sabina and her son James Jr. were now left to care for James H., nearly eighty years old. He declined in health for two more years and ten months. Now came a difficult decision for Sabina. After her husband married Liz, she said she would not live with him. But would Sabina now forgive her husband and take care of him in his ill health? Sabina said she would. She was both wife and nurse to her husband in his last years.

By this time, Sabina was also faced with forgiving a father who had remarried a young woman. How could her beloved mother, Catherina, be so forgotten? There is no evidence she was. John simply said he wanted desperately to have a son carry on his name and his new wife gave him several. After John died, Sabina also struggled with herself to accept the new half-brothers. Family journals make no attempt here to whitewash their history. They all struggled to overcome their differences, as had Emily and Sabina. It took time but the battle was finally won, according to statements made at Sabina's funeral.

She had outlived the other wives, her husband, and all her own family members. In 1919, at age eighty, she was paid a beautiful eulogy by relatives, church members, and friends, including praise by Elder Seymour B. Young, First Council of Seventy, who had known the family for years. He cited her "faith and integrity." Sabina's obituary headline reads: "Faithful Pioneer Woman Buried at Bloomington." It told of her "sublime faith . . . unusual memory and taste for literature and while quiet and unassuming, exercised a strong influence for good . . . raised her family upon the frontier unmurmuringly and with sublime faith and fortitude."

Adina Lloyd said she attended the funeral as a twelve-year old, with her father and her brother Mark. It required a lengthy train trip and horse and sleigh ride from Preston, Idaho, to Bloomington. "But she had been such a wonderful mother and grandmother and friend, we had to go. Everyone treasured her memory."

In the late 1990s, granddaughters Jocelyn Hart Faux and Arlette Hart Day made a pilgrimage to London to locate Sabina's birthplace. They reported, "We were able to see the luxury she left behind. We came away even more amazed at the courage and sacrifice our grandmother made for the values she believed in."

Sabina Scheib Hart, like many pioneer women of the time, while never memorialized in blazing headlines or towering tributes while alive, was remembered by many for a noble life. Her devotion to what she believed in lives undiminished after death.

NOTES

Faux, Jocelyn Hart. *Our Mayflower Ancestors and Their Descendants*. Fresno: Linrose Publishing, 1994.

Hart, Edward L. *Mormon in Motion*. Provo: Windsor Books, 1978.

Hart, Edward L. Personal interviews, as listed.

Hart family histories and records, including letters from Alfred A. Hart.

Lloyd, Adina Hart. Personal interviews, as listed.

Scheib, Sabina. Original four-page journal, in possession of the author.

Chapter Eleven: Wisdom

ELIZA *and* EMILY PARTRIDGE

"The oppressed must learn how to cope with hate . . . without hating."

Establish the United Order, or Law of Consecration, in Jackson County, Missouri—that was the charge given to Edward Partridge, first bishop of the Church, by Joseph Smith. It would be the centerpiece of the newly-declared Zion.

But by late autumn of 1833, it was clear that the Missouri mobsters were not going to allow a United Order, or for that matter any Mormon, to remain within Jackson County. They also would not wait for an orderly exodus amid mild weather, as had been promised. Instead, during the wintry cold of January, every person who called himself a Mormon was driven from the county.

Among those bearing the cruel brunt of mob violence were Bishop Partridge, his wife, Lydia, and their five daughters: Eliza, Emily, Harriet, Caroline and Lydia.

One thing marked the young lives of these sisters: they had to learn how to cope with this traumatic period by relying on the Lord to change what they could, to accept what they could not, and to gain sufficient wisdom to know the difference. They must, as Latter-day Saint young women, learn how to deal with hate without hating. They learned to receive the love of those who loved them with gratitude and how to have enough left over to share with other exiled Saints. They had to embrace each other for their own survival.

After the cruel expulsion of all Mormon families from "Zion" (Jackson County), these frightened young women did not know the meaning of security or family safety. An enemy could attack them at any time, even in their humble home, a makeshift log shelter hastily put together in the wilderness of Clay County. Roving mobs, or even new enemies, might be anywhere. Emily Partridge, then age seven, wrote, "My little sister screamed out into the night in fear." And there would be more fear to come as the days wore on.

As they grew older, the five maturing girls were supposed to associate with and date only Mormon boys; but they, too, were scattered and persecuted. When encountering a stranger, one didn't know whether to admit being a Mormon, or even whether to give greeting. It was easily the most trying period of persecution Latter-day Saints had ever experienced up to that time. They must live like fugitives from the human race, yet learn to murmur not against their church, its leaders, or even their plight.

But it greatly simplified life for the Partridge girls in one way: there was little consternation about what pretty dress to wear to church. There were no pretty dresses. They were fortunate to find anything to wear. Much of the time, there was not even any church, for mobs might be waiting there.

In one act of youthful chagrin against her mother, Emily was sent to repair a hole in her blue dress and did so with a huge white patch. It was more of a statement than a patch, for, "She felt badly plagued because of her dress." It is also possible, since Edward was the one appointed to distribute material goods under the United Order, that he was careful to make certain his own family was not better clothed, fed, or provided for than the Church members he was called to serve.

Partridge descendent Ruth Louise Partridge wrote of Edward and Lydia's girls that they were harshly denied the rites of most young American women in growing up. They sought to be feminine and attractive but were instead focused on primitive survival. Ruth Louise suggests that "despite any appropriate wearing apparel for her daughters," Lydia noted they were "growing pretty" and being "noticed by the Missouri boys." It would be reprehensible to Edward and Lydia that the sons of mob enemies might pay social visits to their daughters.

If they had been adults, of course, they could have simply told themselves that when the going gets tough, the tough get going. They might have been able to say, as many do in later life, "This too shall pass." But they were, in the beginning of the Missouri ordeal, still children, trying to make sense of the chaos around them. Anyone with children, particularly daughters, knows the challenge in raising them under even normal circumstances. They often seek finery, the attainment of social skills (which may include travel, dining in fine restaurants, and shopping in exclusive stores), the best of schooling, and so on. These were denied the Partridge girls as they grew up. Were gospel teachings enough to make up for such privations?

To make matters worse, by 1838 many previously valiant members of the Church were apostatizing or had been cut off. Excommunicated by now were Oliver Cowdery, "first elder of the church" and Book of Mormon witness, and David Whitmer, another of the three witnesses. Thomas B. Marsh, president of the Quorum of the Twelve, and Orson Hyde, an Apostle, had by now turned against the Church and joined the Missourians in an apparent move to waylay persecution. They were to later rejoin the Church in repentant spirit but for now, even older, seemingly more stable members (including W. W. Phelps) were beginning to question their membership. It must have been a particularly bewildering time for those like the Partridge young women to remain true to their faith.

At age seven, Emily wrote that the sight of her father, tarred and feathered by the mob in Independence, left a terrible memory. She said she did not even recognize her father when he returned home. Caroline wrote: "My father was well off until he became a Mormon, then he was driven from place to place and persecuted. We lived in one poor house after another. . . . In July, 1833, a number of armed men entered our home and took my father away." When he returned, Caroline thought he was an Indian and hid under the bed.

Some hope was nurtured by Mormon families that they might be able to return to Independence for material goods left behind; but by late winter of 1834, all redress or opportunity to recover what had been left behind was given up.

Prayer was their strength. At an early age, these girls had to learn wisdom, how to trust in the Lord, to complain as little as possible, and be a courageous example for their younger siblings and to be as optimistic as circumstances might allow. The younger Partridge girls looked to their older sisters for leadership while the family was under siege. And they, in turn, looked to their parents.

Edward and Lydia showed a confidence and trust for better times to come throughout the ordeal, but it was not as easy for these younger souls with less experience to learn to live almost wholly by faith. It would take time.

We will focus on Eliza and Emily because they were the oldest and were most dutiful in keeping journals and, in many cases, daily diaries, even though none were published. It would not be too much of a stretch to compare Eliza, the chief recorder of daily events in Missouri, to Anne Frank, the diary-keeping Dutch girl who hid from German occupation in Amsterdam during WW II in 1944. But as with Anne, Eliza needed to keep her comments about the enemy a secret from them. Following Boggs's extermination order, Eliza and her entire family would be in danger of losing their lives if they were known to be active Mormons, especially as daughters of Bishop Edward Partridge.

Missouri Governor Lilburn Boggs's Extermination Order of 1838 was ill-timed for any member of The Church of Jesus Christ of Latter-day Saints. But it was an especially difficult period for young Eliza and Emily, the oldest daughters of Edward Partridge, who were just approaching the pivotal period of their mid-teen years.

In general, the Missouri mobsters did not consider Mormon women to be serious combatants; they were not sought out as were the men for extermination. But some female members suffered rape and sexual abuse at the hands of mobbers, while others were simply ignored as simpletons who had married into a strange cult.

One of Emily and Eliza's special challenges was that they believed all that their long-suffering parents had taught them. If Edward had not been such a devout believer, with daughters following in his footsteps, they would probably have been allowed to come and go as they pleased. After all, Edward had but to deny a belief in the Book of Mormon in 1833 to avoid being tarred and feathered. He refused to do so.

Joseph Smith had said of Edward shortly after he was baptized in 1831, "He is a man, like Nathaniel of old, without guile." Edward was never able to convert a single one of his family to the restored Church, nor was Lydia. Yet, they stood unmoved throughout their lifetimes in dedication to the Church.

Edward and Lydia made many sacrifices for their faith. The family had to venture from home to find work in a desperate search for food and sustenance, to associate with peers and, if possible, to regain the normal lifestyle once enjoyed in Painesville, Ohio. There Edward had been a successful hatter.

Eliza wrote in her journal that she boarded thirty miles from home, teaching school among potential Mormon enemies. She went three months not knowing if her family was safe. "Although I didn't see anyone I had ever seen before, the Lord watched over me and returned me safely to my parents again. I was at that time 17 years old."

By 1835, Edward was away on a mission to the Ohio region. Eliza wrote that her father simply placed the family in God's hands. "He was convinced that the Lord had set up a kingdom here on Earth and when the Lord called, he must obey. He showed his faith by his works."

After returning from his mission, Edward was frequently arrested and hauled to various courtrooms and jails for the simple crime of being a Mormon. After finally moving his family safely to Illinois during 1839–40, Edward died at the tender age of forty-six, some say of a broken heart for not being able to establish a United Order in Zion. Of course, mobs had prevented him from doing so. He incurred a lion's share of the mob's wrath because he was a "high profile" Mormon leader, a target of those who sought to expunge the new Church from the face of the earth. This, even though Caldwell County, encompassing Far West, had been designated by the Missouri Legislature as a place that would settle the Mormon "problem."

During all this, Edward's wife Lydia was busy trying to raise little Edward Jr., a toddler, and to support her husband through his many court appearances and trials across Missouri.

In spite of all this, the girls did not complain of being bereft of moral comfort as time went by. When driven from their home in Jackson County, Eliza put it this way: "We traveled three miles and camped on the banks of the river [Missouri] under a high bluff. Rain poured down in torrents." Then this terse addition: "This was the first night I had ever spent out of doors."

The family crossed the Missouri River in January into Clay County, and Edward gathered some logs and stretched a tent over them; there was snow on the ground. Later on, "Father found a miserable old house that we could occupy. He and a brother named John Corrill moved their families into this house." Eliza does not say how many members were in the Corrill family, but there were eight in the Partridge clan. One can well imagine the cooperation needed to house and feed them all in such crowded quarters. It helped that John had been Edward's first counselor and had baptized Eliza.

Caroline complained of poisonous snakes. She does not elaborate; no one was bitten but they were sometimes found among boxes on the dirt floor. Emily wrote of hearing wolves howl. About the exodus from Jackson County, she wrote: "Women and children sallied forth from their gloomy retreat to contemplate with heart-wrenching anguish the ravages of a ruthless mob, in the mangled bodies of their husbands and in the destruction of their houses." Other passages from her diary: "Unprotected by the arm of the law . . . the mob quit whipping and began beating with clubs."

The Partridges were not uneducated rustics. They were refined city folk who were out of their element in even moving to western Missouri. Eliza and Emily's mother, Lydia, wrote that when arriving in Independence she saw an immediate difference between life in Ohio and Missouri. In the latter, "women often went barefoot, children shirtless in backwoods style." There also seemed a leanness of intellect.

During this time, Eliza kept a diary but "destroyed it," according to family historian L. L. Ranney. She suggests that Eliza wrote "too freely," perhaps even placing blame on her parents for joining this unwelcome church. Ranney adds, "Today's followers of church history can only lament the loss of her first thoughts about the Missouri years. They appear to represent the candid but not candy-coated feelings of her child and teen years." Eliza's journals that did survive purging are more upbeat and positive. It is possible that in hindsight she re-evaluated her difficult years and saw some benefit gained by being stretched spiritually. Regardless, Eliza moved to Utah with her mother and sisters and remained an active Latter-day Saint with the others even after her husband, Amasa M. Lyman, was excommunicated for teaching false doctrine.

The girls' feelings as they tried to mature into regular Latter-day Saint women are reflected in these comments within their journals and diaries during the difficult Missouri period.

Said Eliza, explaining conditions in Caldwell County: "The people among whom we had been living began to feel uneasy about us. [Notice the lack of condemnation or bitterness; she is simply stating facts.] Later, she wrote, "We know not what we shall be called to pass through before

Zion is delivered and established; therefore, we have a great need to live near God and always be in strict obedience to his commandments."

Upon fleeing Missouri: "As before, we had to leave most of our belongings behind. The church was scattered with no place of gathering. Harriet and Emily had the ague about a year. I did not have it. I had worn it out."

In the Nauvoo period, Eliza alertly noted that John C. Bennett attempted to take the prophet Joseph Smith's life and make it look like an accident, "But the Lord warned Joseph and he was on guard."

After finding a home in Quincy, then Nauvoo, Emily tried to be positive. She said that the family began to "enjoy happy times." Even after it was clear they would be driven from Nauvoo, Emily could write: "There is nothing in this life too dear to sacrifice for the hope our religion gives us."

Family distress was shown in a journal later written by Caroline who "went into a cornfield to pray for survival." Did the Lord answer Caroline's prayer and deliver the family? History records that all of the family eluded mobs and safely moved to Illinois, although Edward and Harriet died shortly after moving there. Yet mother Lydia was to later write: "My faith never failed me; instead it grew stronger in the latter day work."

Perhaps the question of their faith can be answered more fully by seeing what happened to the Partridge girls in the Nauvoo period. As polygamy was ushered into the Church, both Emily and Eliza, who sought to enter into a union with one honoring his priesthood, exchanged marriage vows with the Prophet Joseph. "Emma gave her consent in the morning to the wedding but changed her mind before nightfall, according to Emily: "Emma not only approved of the marriage but chose my sister and I. We were married in her presence with her full and free consent. But later, Emma said some very hard things."

Eliza added, "We looked upon the covenants we made as sacred . . . but we were cast off." Although still married for time and eternity on record, they were not allowed to consummate their marriage vows. Later, when Joseph was martyred, Eliza and Emily were not even allowed to mourn openly as his wives, a matter Emily lamented openly in her diary.

Later, Emily became one of President Brigham Young's polygamous wives. She was twenty-two to Brigham's forty-six. There could be no doubt that he was one she could draw strength from, he being one of the few priesthood holders she ever grew close to, other than her own father.

However, with Brigham busy with the exodus from Nauvoo, Emily found herself alone once more. This time, carrying a three-month old baby in her arms, she crossed the Mississippi River "searching for a friendly face." Still, in many ways she was better off than the other nine Mormon women who gave birth on Sugar Creek during the flight from Illinois. Emily wrote in a gut-wrenching diary entry, "I took my infant and crossed the river, and was again houseless and homeless in the cold and inclement weather of 1846. I wandered from fire to fire . . . looking for someone I knew. . . . I will not attempt to describe my feelings at this time but cold and hungry I surely was, and the prospects looked rather dismal."

Eliza, traveling with sister Caroline, wrote that she crossed the Mississippi on ice that was "very dangerous." She says she was very cold and uncomfortable but didn't complain because, "We were leaving our enemies and hoped for better times."

When crossing the Missouri River, the sisters became separated from their mother. Eliza says they tried to call across to one another and were worried for the other's safety. She expressed the feeling of all family members at that time: "I hope we shall never be separated again until death."

The family had bonded too closely through their ordeals—in the need to rely on each other and their God—to ever depart from one another. All moved into Millard County, Utah, and lived there until their deaths, leading happy and productive lives in the bonds of the gospel, as attested to in their journals.

When Apostle Amasa M. Lyman was excommunicated from the Church, it forced an even closer union between the Partridge girls and their mother. They were left without husbands, fathers, or any priesthood in the family. (Edward Jr. went on two missions to Hawaii and was gone much of the time.)

Mother Lydia summarized the lives of herself and her girls in 1877 by saying: "I have a desire to bear my testimony to the world of the belief I have in the everlasting gospel which is revealed to us in the last days. I have been a member [of this Church] over 45 years and have never had cause for a doubt to cross my mind as to the truth of the Latter-day work. I was acquainted with Joseph Smith and believed him to be a true prophet of God . . . flesh and blood hath not revealed it unto me but my Father in Heaven."

Perhaps the greatest proof of their testimonies was the service rendered the Church until the end of their lives. All of the family served in positions of leadership in Fillmore or Oak City, Millard County. Partridge descendants remember their heritage every Memorial Day in a family reunion at the Oak City Chapel. All who come there on that day are welcome to a breakfast meal and to share in the history of a beloved family who left such a rich legacy of wisdom for their posterity.

NOTES

The Church of Jesus Christ of Latter-day Saints Archives. Salt Lake City, Utah. (Most pages not numbered, typescript and microfilm, No. MS 2845, Access No. 3887–Arch–88. Note: Eliza's diaries are sometimes listed as "Treasures of Pioneer History." Emily's are sometimes listed as "Diary of a Mormon Girl" and "What I Remember." Edward Jr. journals also available at Brigham Young University Lee Library, Special Collections, handwritten, some sections illegible.

Partridge, Ruth Louise. *Other Drums.* Provo, Utah, self-published.

Partridge, Edward Sr. *Journal.* The Church of Jesus Christ of Latter-day Saints Archives. Salt Lake City, Utah.

Partridge Edward Jr., Eliza, Emily, and Caroline. Diaries and journals.

Ranney, L. L. *Our Priceless Heritage*, parts 1 and 11, self-published, Salt Lake City, Utah, 1959.

Ranney, L. L. Partridge Family News Bulletin. Salt Lake City, Utah, 1957, no longer published.

Smith, Joseph. *History of the Church*, Vol. 1.

Smith, Joseph, et al. *Doctrine and Covenants.* Also known as *Book of Commandments.* Salt Lake City: Deseret Book, 1833.

Wixom, Hartt. *Edward Partridge, First Bishop of the Church of Jesus Christ of Latter-day Saints.* Springville: Cedar Fort, 1998.

Chapter Twelve: Integrity

EZRA TAFT BENSON

"Lowering my standards would not attract me at any figure."

Ezra Taft Benson, thirteenth president of The Church of Jesus Christ of Latter-day Saints, did not live in the pioneer era as those in the other stories included did. However, he was born before the twentieth century (4 August 1899) and was in that sense a nineteenth-century (pioneer) fore-bearer.

His great grandfather, Ezra T. Benson, was a new convert in Nauvoo who was selected by Brigham Young to replace the excommunicated Hiram Page in the Quorum of the Twelve. Benson told in later years how he wrestled with the devil, rebuked him, and called on God for a testi-mony—which he received. Young Ezra Taft Benson often told how he tried to live up to the examples set by his parents, particularly his name-sake, Ezra T. Benson.

Ezra Taft Benson, the thirteenth president of the Church, nobly rep-resented the principle of integrity. Integrity is defined in Webster as "unity of purpose, wholeness, completeness." The 2003 priesthood and Relief Society manual gives greater meaning: "Integrity means faithfully living by principles of truth and righteousness."

Yet, once as a high school student Ezra was labeled by his principal as a cheat, and his examination paper was thrown away. "It was the only time my integrity was ever brought into question," said Ezra 65 years later; it was an incident he never forgot.

More than any Church leader, Benson was thrust into a public arena where he was expected to be one of the boys, join the crowd, toast with cocktails, talk the tough language of politics, and fit in to Washington society as Secretary of Agriculture in President Dwight D. Eisenhower's cabinet. Instead, he stood out because he refused to abandon the principles he had grown up with. Ironically, his rise to prominence was due to one thing—he just kept on being who he was: Ezra Taft Benson, a farm kid from the little Mormon town of Whitney, Idaho.

Why quit being who you are if it is what got you there?

Ezra was so much "the farm boy from Idaho" that he resisted a tradition (indeed a mandate) from Washington protocol that he and his children be chauffeured wherever they went, including to and from school. The Benson children, reflecting their upbringing, were embarrassed; they asked to be let off a block away from the school yard so they would not be seen appearing to be better than their peers.

Benson knew he was moving into a hornet's nest as Secretary of Agriculture. Farmers had come to distrust big government, while at the same time more and more demanded a handout from it. A revolution was in the making. Rural folk were tired of being represented by political hacks who offered "favors" for some under a spoils system. Benson knew he had been selected because he would administer "agricultural justice" to all. He was a "dirt farmer," a "sod buster" who understood agriculture and was expected to throw out the politics. That included not doing for farmers what they could do for themselves, a firm belief of both President Eisenhower and, back home, Church President David O. McKay.

Due to high price supports (and the government buying surplus products from the farmers), so much had accumulated in Washington that there was little room to store it all. When Ezra took office in January of 1953, the government owned thirty-seven million pounds of butter, seven million pounds of cheese, and fifty-six million pounds of dried milk, plus so many tons of cotton and wheat that it cost $66.9 million in 1953 to store it all. Clearly, something had to be done.

Ezra Taft Benson was the man to do it. Yet, "Ike" had promised farmers high level price supports for at least another year, although Benson believed that only in times of emergency or unforeseen disaster should government step in to bail them out. He believed that farmers should prosper by hard work, not by dependency, which would weaken their self-will and make them slaves to government whim. Benson preached this philosophy wherever he went: "You cannot help people permanently by doing for them what they can do for themselves. I had to help the people stand on their own two feet." The idea was not new. Joseph Smith had long preached that he taught people correct principles and that they could then govern themselves.

Benson eventually lowered price supports and got the nation's farmers, for the most part, to put confidence in his program and give it a chance to work. It took time.

In addition, Benson had promised to cut waste; some 78,000 employees in the U. S. Department of Agriculture grew uneasy. How many would lose their jobs? Not an appreciable number as it turned out, although the new Secretary made it clear he expected a full day's work for a full day's pay.

It seemed inevitable that Benson's courageous stance would be verbally attacked. He was the target of angry egg-tossers during a speaking tour in South Dakota. Mid-West farmers sent letters to the editor, complaining about lowered hog price supports. Nevertheless, one thing even his enemies agreed on: Ezra Taft Benson never backed off what he believed to be right. He was known for honesty among friend and foe alike.

Despite all the adversity, Benson watched Eisenhower get re-elected— proof enough that Benson was not a liability. In fact, it was an indication that the nation's once murmuring Grangers were beginning to see the value of the agricultural iconoclast's tough farm philosophy.

Benson was so well-known for his integrity that at the time of his death at age ninety-four, he was the front page story of the St. Louis Post-Dispatch on 31 May 1994. The article enumerated his many achievements, focusing particularly on his honesty.

The newly-elected Eisenhower had never met Benson when he selected him to fill the secretarial post. But Ike was aware of the Idahoan's adherence to principle (along with his knowledge of grass roots agriculture). In his autobiography, Eisenhower, dwelling on his years as Commander in Chief of Allied Forces in the war against Germany and Axis Powers, wrote that his commander, General Marshall, always chose men to work under him who could be implicitly trusted to keep their word, were not self-promoters and did not seek self-aggrandizement, were positive about getting the job done, and did not pass the buck to others. It is not a stretch to believe that Ike sought men to serve under him with similar qualities, both as a military general and later as U.S. president.

As mentioned earlier, however, Benson was once branded by a high school principal as a cheater. It was to have a profound impact on his life. The incident was recalled sixty-five years later (1979) in a letter written to Newell Hart, editor of the Cache Valley Newsletter in Preston, Idaho. To my knowledge, this letter has never before been made public in any form (including several excellent biographies of Benson) outside this singular epistle.

At the time he wrote it, Benson was President of the Quorum of the Twelve. Newell Hart, not even a member of the Church, was so thrilled to receive the letter for a monthly edition of his newsletter that he ran the entirety of it. Benson's letter started out reminiscing about a name mentioned by Hart, a Henry Mockli who was Ezra's neighbor in Whitney, just east of Preston. Ezra then refers to a Joseph A. Geddes thus:

> The only time I can remember having my integrity questioned was in high school in an examination. Joseph Geddes was the principal of the Oneida Stake Academy.
>
> I believe the examination was in economics. Brother Geddes had the habit of standing at the back of the room, watching the students during an examination. I was writing rather vigorously when the lead of my pencil broke.
>
> I asked my neighbor across the aisle to let me borrow his pocket knife. As he handed me the knife, Brother Geddes came down the aisle and said, "Hand in your paper, and you'll not be permitted to play in the basketball game tonight."
>
> I was one of the leading forwards. I explained I was just asking for his knife so I could sharpen my pencil, but no explanation would satisfy him.

It was a dispirited young man who stopped on his way home that afternoon to check his "string of traps" on Worm Creek. Yes, it seems Ezra Taft Benson was learning economic independence early by trapping muskrats, skinning the pelts himself, stretching them over a shingle and sending them to Chicago for payment. He added, "This project kept me in spending money for books and other things." Benson said he went home and "told my father what happened. He felt sure that I was honest."

Ezra was later out milking the cows when a telephone call came from Coach Charlie Cutler that "I should come over to the gymnasium that evening, that the president would see me. . . . President Geddes . . . asked me if I would confess my dishonesty, to which I replied, 'I have not been dishonest. There is nothing to confess.'"

Coach Cutler apparently prevailed upon President Geddes, however, to let the young man play anyway. Still, the cloud of suspicion hung heavily over his head. Ezra "went into the game with very little spirit and we lost the game. I've never forgotten this incident."

 Benson, sixty-seven years after the fact, may have hoped to send a message to Geddes, who was still alive at that time. Ezra wrote Hart, "I am pleased he [Geddes] is still with us." Benson may have been willing to forgive, but it was not easy to forget this early blemish against his name. Yet, to his credit, Ezra did not use it as an excuse for possible failure, nor hold it against the Church both he and Geddes belonged to.

Benson went on to explain in the newsletter how important basketball was to him and his peers in southern Idaho. He had a basketball standard in his yard and practiced between farm chores. His father and mother took a great interest in basketball; they had seven sons who played the game. Benson says the only time he ever heard his father swear was at a game where he, Ezra, missed a foul pitch. "Father yelled out, "Dammit, T, put it in." Ezra explained that he was always called "T" as a boy—"my middle initial. I think my father was happier than any of us when we won that game by one point."

So intense was the fever for basketball that in one game at Shelley, Idaho, when the home team apparently had no basketball court, the swimming pool was drained and hoops were put up on either end. There was no out of bounds. "I shall never forget that game, especially when the two centers who were running for the ball collided and both of them were knocked out."

Ezra was most impressed, however, by a Rexburg team that were "fine losers." He said, "They hitched a beautiful team of fine Percherons to a bob sleigh and drove us to Sugar City the next evening. I drove the team most of the way. I have always received more of a thrill from a good team of horses than I have from the finest automobile."

Benson signed off with, "This is a long letter. I hope you will not feel obligated to use any of it."

The request, of course, went unheeded.

I had an occasion to learn more about the man Benson in two ways. I was present when he gave the funeral oration at the death of my grandfather, Arthur W. Hart, who was also the Franklin County prosecuting attorney and the Benson family lawyer for twenty-eight years, Also, Benson grew up near a cousin, Marilyn Nash Hull, and her husband Gib, from Whitney and nearby Cub River. The Hulls's premature baby is buried near Benson's grave marker in the Whitney cemetery.

To Gib: "What kind of person was he?"

"As advertised," said Hull. "Honest as a summer day is long. With a reputation for work from dawn to dark. When he became Secretary of Agriculture, he was no figurehead. He had pitched hay and thinned sugar beets with the best of them. He had waged a war on weeds just like any farm kid. No one knew the challenge of farm life better than he did."

It was both his love of farming and his trustworthiness that led Benson to the highest post in national government that any Mormon has yet attained. From being a model dairyman and farmer, he became Franklin County Agricultural Agent, then Extension Specialist at the University of Idaho, then Executive Secretary of the National Council of Farmers Cooperatives, till he was eventually asked by President Eisenhower to serve as U. S. Secretary of Agriculture.

Benson's reputation for honesty had earlier been noted by the First Presidency of the Church. Ezra Taft Benson was a "man for all seasons" who would not be deterred from God's program on earth. Benson was called to the Quorum of the Twelve and later served as its president. He was called to be President of The Church of Jesus Christ of Latter-day Saints at the death of a man he dearly loved, Spencer W. Kimball, in November 1985. On 30 August 1989, Benson received the U.S. Presidential Citizen's Medal from President George Bush "for a lifetime of dedicated service to Country, Community, Church and Family." Benson served as Prophet of the Church until his death on 30 May 1994.

However, there was one incident in this rise to higher responsibility that was pivotal to Benson's achievements. It was a test that, had he failed, might have restricted him to a life of hum-drum service and, possibly, mediocrity. When being sought to serve as Executive Secretary of NCFC in Washington, Ezra established the keynote to his life in national service with this statement: "I told them plainly of my standards, activities in the Church and advised them that any job which would require the lowering of those standards would not attract me at any figure. To my joy [they told me] . . . that one reason they'd come to me was because of my ideals." Benson made it clear that "if this job in Washington will entail buying influence and good will by providing cocktails. . . . I am not interested."

He had passed the test with the highest of honors. He was told the committee selecting him had been checking him out for a year, was aware of his standards, "and would be greatly disappointed" if he was to let down his lofty ideals.

Benson was one of the Church's great missionaries. Like Wilford Woodruff, the previous president of the Church, Benson served a mission in England, a country plentiful with converts to the faith. Although Benson didn't match Woodruff's mark of baptizing thousands (Woodruff's journal shows he organized fifty-one branches of the Church in England), Benson influenced many to look favorably upon the Church. He reached thousands through his work, and his post as U. S. Secretary of Agriculture took him around the world, allowing him to meet with kings and leaders of many countries. In addition, Benson spent much time overseas helping administer the welfare program of the Church and allowing people to see firsthand that the Church could be counted on to help the impoverished and needy, honestly; not all "charitable" organizations for relief had earned that reputation. As a member of the United States Cabinet, Benson's example helped others to look favorably upon The Church of Jesus Christ of Latter-day Saints. His influence carried far beyond the Utah and American borders. Up to his time, probably no Mormon exerted more influence over a wider area of the world than Ezra Taft Benson.

President Benson often said in general conference priesthood sessions, "May the devil miss you." That statement could have more implications than at first thought. Sins of omission, as well as commission, come to mind. He urged all within sound of his voice to keep an honest course.

Benson always served as an example of what can be accomplished by simply living the principles of the gospel, even in the spotlight. But the thing that stamped Ezra Taft Benson as a great man more than anything else was his determination to live by the principle of integrity—even if no one was watching.

NOTES

Dew, Sheri L. *Ezra Taft Benson: A Biography*. Salt Lake City: Deseret Book, 1987

Eisenhower, Dwight D. *Crusade in Europe*. New York: Doubleday, 1948.

Hart, Reed. *Let's Talk, It's Good for the Soul*. Salt Lake City: Hawkes Publishing, 1995.

Hart, Newel. self-published "Cache Valley Newsletter," Preston, Idaho. (Newsletter no longer published.)

Knight, Hal, and Stan Kimball. *111 Days to Zion, The Day to Day Trek of the Mormon Pioneers*. Salt Lake City: Big Moon Traders, 1997.

Woodruff, Wilford. *Journal*, edited by M.F. Cowley. Salt Lake City: Deseret Book, 1909.

About the Author

Hartt Wixom, 74, has been a lifelong student of pioneer and Church history. His love of history has taken him to many sites of interest from Palmyra, Independence, Far West, and Nauvoo to the Mormon, Oregon, and California trails throughout the Rocky Mountains and West Coast. He has written many newspaper and magazine articles about these events, winning regional and national awards for "unbiased writing and reporting."

His books include biographies of frontier legend Jacob Hamblin and the first bishop of the Church, Edward Partridge.

Wixom taught at Brigham Young University in the department of communications for fourteen years and has done extensive postgraduate work in history at the University of Utah. Tutors included veteran historians Charles Peterson, Davis Bitton, and David Miller.

Because of his fascination with how the past has made the present possible, he intends to continue "exploring historical places, studying the events, and ferreting out stories of people who made a difference."